FROM RAGE TO
REDEMPTION

The Tragic & Inspirational Life
of J. David Norcott, Jr.

THOMAS MARTIN

Wasteland Press

Shelbyville, KY USA
www.wastelandpress.net

From Rage to Redemption:
The Tragic & Inspirational Life of J. David Norcott, Jr.
by Thomas Martin

First Printing – February 2022
ISBN: 978-1-68111-451-4
Cover Design by Brian Hirakami
Cover Photograph by H.B. Wise

Printed in the U.S.A.

0   1   2   3   4

Someone said to me, "I don't know how you do it."
I replied, "I wasn't given a choice."

People ask how I can stay so positive after losing my legs.
I simply ask how they stay so negative with theirs.
– Sgt. Johnny Joey Jones

DEDICATION

For David

ACKNOWLEDGEMENTS

I would like to thank the following people for their help, inspiration, and contributions to this very special project:

H.B. Wise
Kat Occhipinti
Steve Blackman & Gottlieb
Bill Shipe
Barbara Peznowski
Cecil Bacher
Joseph D. Norcott, Sr.
Judge Edward Kinkaede
Joey Goss
Kathy Johnston
Andrew & Glenda Bashor
Mark Ashford
Tony Occhipinti
Renee Lee Ann Franklin
Sally Hoffman
Sara Franke
Barbara Katzka
Mark Taylor
Nick Vujicic

TABLE OF CONTENTS

INTRODUCTION

I met Joseph David Norcott, Jr. (David) through a mutual friend, H.B. Wise, in the spring of 2016. HB's company photographs 5K and 10K foot races. It was at one such race where HB first met David. In talking to him and hearing his story, HB felt the two of us should meet. Before the meeting, HB gave me a very brief synopsis of David's story and invited me to lunch. Since I had been through my own health and medical trials and had written a book, HB felt I might be helpful in getting David moving in the right direction to write his story as well.

I drove to the race, unsure of this meeting. As it was raining, I parked and joined HB in his truck. While sitting and talking, David came ambling over to us on his prosthetic legs. My first impulse was to jump out of the car to help him. He seemed to be doing fine on his own, though, not really needing any help.

Here I sat, now facing one of my worst fears. As a child, when I became insufferably whiney, my mother, who grew up during the Great Depression, would calmly tell me to put on my shoes. She then said we would be going to the County Hospital where she wanted me to meet children born with no arms or legs. After meeting them, I was then to tell her how "difficult" my generally privileged life really was.

Because of this, I developed a tremendous fear of County Hospitals and anyone missing their limbs.

Now here, on this day, I am to meet David Norcott, amputee. I sucked up what courage I could muster, got out of the car and hesitantly shook his right hand, a hand clearly missing its small finger. My instinct was to flee, yet we had all agreed to have lunch together. I was not about to be that whiney boy my mother disdained. I bucked up and we drove to the restaurant.

At lunch I was uncomfortably able to look David in the face while his prosthetic legs were hidden beneath the table top. I offered any help he might need in writing his book and I provided him with my card.

I left hoping this was my last meeting with David. I felt I had done my part, I had offered my help, and it was now up to him to act. I could go home with a clean conscience.

As the Jewish saying goes: "Man plans, God laughs."

Within a couple of weeks, God made me very aware of His plans. He repeatedly nudged me to pick up the phone and call David to meet for lunch. With great trepidation, I picked it up and called. David agreed to the lunch and we set a place and time to meet.

God, not wanting this to be easy on me, put me in the most awkward of situations. When David and I sat down to talk, David looked directly into my eyes and said, "So Tom, how can I help you?"

Damn – God had provided me with the "what" but not the "why." I had made the phone call, I had arranged the lunch, what God had not provided was the reason for the meeting. I looked mutely at David and was completely unsure of what to say. In that moment I didn't even know why I was there.

After a long, awkward pause, I told him I just thought it would be a good idea for us to meet and I again offered any help he might want in writing his book.

At this point, David did not seem overly interested, although I know the idea intrigued him in some way. "hmmm...." I thought, "maybe the timing just isn't yet right."

One of my avocations, at this point in my life, is speaking and fundraising for Canine Companions for Independence (CCI). CCI breeds, raises, and trains dogs to help persons with physical and emotional challenges. Wondering if this would be a good match, I asked David if he had ever considered a service dog.

His response took me aback. As a dog lover, I expected him to respond with enthusiasm. Instead, he responded with an overly firm "NO!" I knew I had just stuck my foot in my mouth but I did not know why.

I quickly realized I was absolutely the wrong person to whom he should speak about this.

I thought about the different CCI graduates I had met and recalled a moving speech from Mr. Steve Blackman, a US Veteran who had been seriously injured in a training accident. I arranged for David to meet Steve and his CCI service dog Gottlieb. They spoke for a short time and the very next day David texted me saying he had applied online for a service dog from CCI.

Roughly 10 months later, David was part of the February 2017 graduating class at the CCI regional center in Las Colinas, Texas.

David, and his service dog Kinsey, often go with me to speak to groups about CCI. One day, driving back from a speaking engagement, David told me that earlier in the day he had treated himself to a manicure. Without thinking, I replied, "I prefer a pedicure over a manicure." Dripping with sarcasm, David replied, "Why thank you, Tom. That's good to know." Realizing the outrageous faux pas (pun intended) I had just made, I turned to him and said, "Well, I guess I have finally reached the point where you are no longer 'David the amputee' to me, you are now just 'David.' I apologize now for anything stupid I may say in the future."

In June of 2018 I again approached David about my writing his biography. This time, he was more receptive and agreed to the project. In retrospect, I don't think he really believed I would actually sit down and make it all happen, so it was a rather safe bet for him.

As the writing progressed, we talked of speaking opportunities and how he could promote the book. As I asked around, I discovered that I had many second-hand contacts to people who might be able to get David in front of crowds of up to tens of thousands of people. I think this both thrilled and terrified David and it was about at that time that progress on the book took a sudden turn

I finally became impatient, waiting for David to write his book. I wanted to see it published, I wanted others to know his story, and I wanted people to meet David on the same level that I had been able to know him. So, one day in June 2018, I offered to actually write this book, to move the project along and finish it.

As you read this book, please keep in mind that it is written from David's perspective and therefore is in first person, present tense. So, you the reader, will only learn things as David learns them. Also realize that for the first two sections of the book, David is on a wide array of drugs that dull his mind and reasoning.

One other thing, for those unfamiliar with amputation and prosthetic legs, know that a below-the-knee amputation is far easier for the patient to recover and use prosthetics than an above-the-knee amputee.

Writing this book was quite the journey for me and it had a most unexpected ending. In the Epilogue, I will tell you my challenges in writing this book and working with David.

As a caveat, I want to be clear that I have written this story as it was told to me by David. I have done no fact checking save to interview some of the people mentioned in the story. From these interviews and my own observations, I suspect that the vast bulk of the story is true.

I was inspired by David's story for many reasons. Mostly, I found it to be the story of all men, merely at an extreme. I was especially taken by David saying that "normal" life is actually quite boring and routine, and that he had to simply accept and live with that fact. His life is a living story of the old saying, "Most men lead lives of quiet desperation." David's amazingly inspirational life ranges from falling into the deepest of life's abysses and pulling himself up by his bootstraps to his rising above the mire and despair.

PART I:
RAGE

"Be still,
and know that I am God."
– Psalms 46:10

"Don't be afraid…
There is a plan;
there is always a plan"
– Mr. Jordan, *Heaven Can Wait*

CHAPTER 1:
September 3, 1998

I am flying down the highway in the dark, my car going well over 90 miles an hour on a clear, warm Texas summer night. I am strung out on the most powerful emotion, the most powerful drug known to man: Rage.

Actually, I don't even know how fast I am speeding, my foot pressing the gas pedal as far as it will go. I barrel down Eagle Mountain, just north of Fort Worth, on Boat Club Road winding toward the intersection with Ten Mile Bridge Road.

I am putting myself in the most dangerous of situations because of one of the most foolish of reasons. Earlier in the day, my girlfriend and I fought on the phone. I would like to say it was over something important, but it was not. It was about her cat. Not one to lose an argument and already angry, I got into my car and drove to her house on Eagle Mountain. We continued the argument with tremendous voracity. My anger escalated to rage, reaching a level that consumed all reason as well as any emotion other than the rage. As a final, emphatic gesture, I picked up a small table in her house and threw it through her sliding glass patio door. I am not even human when I leave her house, I am rage and I am *only* rage I march out of her house, get in my car and head home.

Still fuming, I barrel down the hill. As I come around a bend in my black Chevrolet Monte Carlo, at too high of a speed, I over-correct. Doing so causes me to veer into the painted median of the road. So filled with rage, I simply do not care. I am taking on the world, I am its master and I am invincible! Nothing can hurt me; nothing can stop me.

I am wrong.

Another car, also driving at a high, unsafe speed is coming directly at me in the median. She too, is going too fast and is also no longer in control of her car.

We collide, head on. The crack of the impact is so intense that Jan Robertson and her husband, living up the street, run out of their house to investigate. They arrive at the accident and find my mangled, burned and bleeding body trapped within what is left of my car. They immediately call 911 for help.

I am clinically dead, gratefully unaware of the extreme damage to my body and the knowledge of what is happening around me.

In a short while, the fire department arrives. The paramedic rushes over to my car. He does a brief assessment while the firefighters work to extract my limp body. The paramedic determines that I am dead, that my injuries are not compatible with life and decides **it is not worth his time** trying to resuscitate me. He leaves me to attend to those in the other car.

This *should* be the end of my story, the end of my life, but God has other plans.

Interestingly, my career is that of a paramedic. I am employed by both MedStar and the Tarrant County hospital district (which also serves the county jail).

Very shortly thereafter an ambulance arrives and its paramedic, Cecil Bacher, comes over to me. Cecil is also an employee of MedStar.

In attending to me, he finds my MedStar badge. Realizing that I am a co-worker, he ignores the hopelessness of the situation and works to resuscitate me. I have neither a pulse nor am I breathing. Cecil can see that my right lower leg is badly mangled and sees that I have burns over much of my body. He knows it is unlikely I can be saved, but a spark inside of him keeps him moving, doing the job he has been trained to do – save lives. Miraculously, he *is* able to resuscitate me. My body, though, is so badly damaged that each time he brings me back to life, I quickly return to death. This ballet continues even after he radios for assistance and a helicopter arrives to transport me from the scene.

I am blissfully unaware of just how many times I die that night.

Now I fly over the lights of Dallas, Texas to Parkland Hospital. Parkland is the very same hospital where President John Kennedy was taken after being shot in Dealey Plaza.

CHAPTER 2:
Parkland Hospital, Dallas
September 4, 1998 to March 1999

I arrive at Parkland Hospital unconscious, hovering between life and death. I do not know what has happened to me or what is now happening, but even without my participation, the drama continues.

I arrive with my right leg badly mangled, my lungs collapsed, my thorax filled with blood, a head trauma which includes hemorrhaging (internal bleeding), spinal cord swelling, Aortic aneurysm, fractures on all long bones, burns on my legs, pelvis and torso, and damage to my spleen and several other internal organs. As the first paramedic surmised, I have injuries not consistent with life.

The doctors confirm this to my family, "there is no real scientific reason why David is even alive." The trauma and damage my body has sustained should indicate only death. Yet, I *am* alive. The doctors also warn my parents that there is no way to know who I might be if I regain consciousness. Because of the traumatic brain injury, caused when my head hit the steering wheel of my car, they do not know if my brain will even function. My parents, grateful I am alive, now must live with the angst of not knowing if their son will return to them or if I will live out my days as a vegetable.

My right leg has burns down to the marrow below the knee and gangrene develops. My dear sister, Holly, is put in the most difficult situation of her life. Since I am unconscious, she must sign the paperwork authorizing the amputation of my right leg just above the knee. She is understandably traumatized by this, but there is no one else to perform the task. She follows the advice of the medical team and signs the authorization. *With that signature, though, comes horrific, long-term guilt.*

During the amputation surgery, they also do burn debridement, a procedure where burned, dead flesh is removed to allow new tissue to form. Along with the debridement they apply skin grafts on the more devastatingly burned areas. They then insert a rod into my left leg in an attempt to save it.

"I was able to watch one of the burn debridement. In spite of David being in a medically induced coma, I could still see him screaming in pain."

I am constantly kept either in a medically-induced coma or under heavy sedation, but in spite of this, I have a very vivid dream one morning shortly after the surgery. I am standing on a dock over a lake when a massive storm approaches. The dock begins to pitch up and down, and yaw left to right. Suddenly, in a scene of Biblical proportions, an enormous fish jumps from the lake and swallows me.

The old David is gone.

The old David may be gone but God has laid a new plan and a new path. A plan only He can envision and make manifest. The new David is in His hands now.

For me, I merely float in an ocean of medication.

I believe in God, but have never had a close relationship with Him.

Yet, as God saw His divine plan using an imperfect Moses as His spokesman, so does He have a plan for David, regardless of David's current level of faith.

After the amputation surgery, I develop Acute Respiratory Distress Syndrome: fluid leaks into my lungs making it difficult or even impossible for me to breathe. Because of this, my blood oxygen levels fall. This is a fairly common problem in critically ill patients and can be lethal. The treatment is to give me enough oxygen and wait; wait while my body heals the cause of the fluid leak.

To add to my growing number of problems, because of my burns I develop Pseudomonas, a bacterial infection common in burn patients. They try controlling the infection through IV antibiotics, but while treating it, a Methicillin-Resistant Staphylococcus Aureus (MRSA) infection is unleashed. MRSA is a virulent infection and once it takes hold it is very difficult to eradicate or control.

With these two infections, I am now under what is called "reverse precautions." This means that anyone entering my room must don a gown, mask and gloves and there is a secondary door through which they must pass.

I am a mess; what more can I say?

In spite of this, God's hand is upon me. With His help and the help of my doctors, each challenge is slowly overcome. God is clearly looking out for me. I realize He has been orchestrating events even weeks prior to the accident. He has been placing people in my life to help ease some of the pain I am currently experiencing and also easing long-held pain from my childhood. Only one week prior to the accident, I helped move my parents and my sister from the Washington, D.C. area to Texas. In fact, their moving van is still sitting in the parking lot of my apartment complex. Instead of being alone in Texas, I have my family to provide emotional support as I face this next chapter in my life.

I awake after approximately twelve weeks in Parkland. I have no idea where I am, what has happened or what is currently happening. My parents are with me as I am wheeled down a long hallway. They tell me I am at Parkland. Being relatively new to Texas myself, this name has no meaning to me. From the treatment I am receiving, I think Parkland must be some sort of resort or spa.

I am wheeled into a room, undressed, and a team of nurses begin bathing me. Yes, I do like this place! Never have I been pampered to this degree. But my foggy mind drifts to why I am here. Worried, suddenly, about the cost of such a place, I say to my parents, "Don't let Tony and Jen pay for this. I have money in my checking account." Tony is my long-time, best friend and Jen is his wife. Since they are financially comfortable, I wrongly assume they are paying for this luxurious treatment I am receiving.

After the bath, I am carefully dried and placed into a very soft bed, a bed designed for burn patients. It is all so wonderful! It seems strange to me, but I am far too drugged to over think the situation and see no reason to protest. I decide to relax and merely enjoy the experience.

The bed is wonderfully soft, but because of both the burns to my skin and my head injury, I am not permitted to control it. So, I can neither raise nor lower the bed, I am permitted only to lie flat. Neither am I given a call button for the nursing staff or control of the TV. Actually, there may be a call button somewhere on the bed, but I am not aware of it.

My dad (well, I think it is my dad), decides the time is right and tells me I was in a car accident and that my right leg has been amputated. Through the haze of drugs, I understand what he is telling me, but I am unable to fully process or accept the news. Continuing their attempts to save my left leg, the staff comes in and applies a brace.

Back in my room in the burn unit, I am vexed by the temperature. The room is always either too hot or too cold. I am rather warm-blooded by nature and prefer a cooler ambient temperature. The warmth of the room makes me uncomfortable and cranky. This is a symptom specific to my own TBI.

Through some serious complaining on my part, the nurses are kind enough to come in, lay towels on my naked body, and place ice on top of the towels. I am in heaven! The coolness seeps down to my skin and it is wonderful. For a short while I am very comfortable and relaxed.

Nights are the most difficult; whether it is the drugs or repressed memories of the accident, I do not know, but I awake crying and screaming. Because of the double doors into my room, the nurses cannot hear my cries for help. Usually, the reasons for my screams are completely illogical, but because of the injuries to my head and brain *and* the constant cocktail of drugs I am given, I can rarely think in a linear fashion. Sometimes my cries are simply over the constant noise from the television. I cannot seem to equate using the television control to actually *controlling* the television. So, in the midst of my frustration, I pick up the phone and ask them to call my dad.

My relationship with my father has not always been the best. He was born in New York City but grew up in a boy's home in South Carolina. He is a crusty alpha-male type man who never seemed to have much empathy for anyone. When the two of us were in a room together, it was like two male dogs circling, each looking for an advantage to strike.

Yet, now, in my darkest hour of need, my father heeds my calls; even after a long work shift, he gets out of bed, dresses and drives the 40 minutes from his home in Fort Worth to Parkland to see me. This doesn't just happen once, it happens night after night. Each time I call, he responds. When he arrives, he finds me crying or screaming. My perception of him having no empathy is forever changed. I finally see the man beneath the crusty exterior and I thank God he is here for me.

During the day, my father is at work, so instead I call my friends Tony and Jen. Interestingly, both Tony and I are paramedics and work for MedStar. Answering my calls, Tony and/or Jen make the one-hour drive from Granbury to Parkland to sit with me and calm me. God is providing me with comfort, preparing me for what my new life will be.

Since the calls I make are collect, Tony and Jen buy me a calling card on which to charge the calls, it being much cheaper than the constant collect calls. Thankfully, in spite of my usual confusion, I am able to understand how to use the card and my friends continue responding to my anxious pleas.

Even though I have only lived in Texas for about one year, I am overwhelmed by the outpouring of love from my few friends and co-workers. My supervisor at Medstar, Pat Knight, comes to visit me regularly and since his wife is a nurse at Parkland, she stops by often as well. Co-workers from the jail also come to visit. After a life filled mostly with anger and resentment, I am very slowly learning gratitude. God is molding and tempering me.

One other thing that comforts me is a picture placed in my room on the wall. It is a picture of Kyle, my four-year-old son who lives with my estranged wife in Maryland. On many dark days, I look up at this picture and I am able to pull myself together. Someday, somehow, I will be his father again.

In spite of all of the discomforts and challenges, I wake one morning knowing that somehow everything will be alright. The source of the epiphany is that I awake with an erection. At this point, I still do not even fully understand the extent of my injuries; even though I have been told that my leg has been removed. Yet, the fact I have an erection makes me feel alive again. Yes, ladies, men really are this simple.

I have a surprise visitor today. I hear the door open and see my girlfriend enter. She walks to my bed, looks me over and says a few awkward pleasantries. It is quite uncomfortable for both of us. I am sure we are both wracked with guilt and with "what if" scenarios. "What if she didn't bring up the issues with her cat?" "What if I hadn't driven up to her house?" "What if she didn't let me leave?" Any one of a hundred things would have led to a very different outcome. I, of course, cannot keep replaying "What if" scripts in my mind. The damage is done and I must live with it.

Her visit is short. With the guilt she likely carries, I suspect this will be her one and only visit.

Her visit makes me also consider my estranged wife. I know we are separated, but I cannot help but wonder if I might hear from her. Would this accident provoke a response and even a call? I doubt it, but it would still be nice.

It is nearly impossible to be modest in a hospital if you are a long-term patient. As I lay naked in my soft bed, the daily procession of staff comes to care for me. Parkland is a teaching hospital affiliated with UT Southwestern University. During the day the parades of doctors, whom I refer to as "The Penguin Squads," regularly march in and give me the once over. Even though I am on a steady diet of anti-depressants, anti-seizure medications, pain killers and mood stabilizers the quantity of drugs I am given doesn't take away the discomfort of being so fully on display to so many people.

As soon as I think there is nothing else that can embarrass me, something new happens. Today, as I am being bathed, I ask my nurse for a urinal. She looks at me and says, "Just go ahead and pee, we are cleaning you up anyway." So, with an audience watching, I let loose. That not being awkward enough, it is at that very moment that one of Penguin Squads arrives. So, there I lay, naked to the world, with a stream of urine shooting from my pecker as the team of doctors stands watching. Yep, I can still be embarrassed.

Back in the burn unit, physical therapy (PT) begins teaching me how to roll over in bed. Again, while I am completely naked, so now even more people get to see the "real" David Norcott. I have many wonderful nurses and therapists, but this morning a radiant woman walks into my room. I do not know her name, but she looks exactly like the image of Aunt Jemima on a box of pancake mix. I decide to call her Jenny.

I quickly realize that Jenny is actually my "tough love" nurse. Unlike most of the staff, who coddles me, Jenny is here to help me progress. Jenny first orders me to roll over. I look up at her and say, "I can't, it is far too painful."

Jenny looks down at me, scowls, and firmly says, "'Can't' ain't a word I ever want to hear from you again, Suga', you need to just dig in and do it!"

As I shriek in pain, Jenny continues riding my ass by saying, "Just push through the pain, you can do it!" She treats me as if I am her child, not merely her patient. I curse her, under my breath of course, but I also know she has my best interest at heart. She is rebuilding my grit and my determination as much as she is helping me rebuild my body. Her tough love makes the days ahead much easier.

Through these various angels, God is also working to rebuild and reshape my soul.

The day comes when I start learning to use a wheelchair. The first thing I learn is how to get out of my bed and into the chair. There are several physical therapists here to help me, but one especially catches my eye. She is full figured and quite buxom. She takes the lead helping me out of my bed and into the wheelchair.

As this is happening, I realize my core body strength is gone, atrophied from my time lying in the hospital bed. So once in the wheelchair, I find I cannot sit up on my own. As my body is released from the hands of my PT, my torso and arms simply fall. I fall forward, face first, into those lovely, full breasts.

I am horribly embarrassed but she calmly tells me it is no big deal and not to worry about it. Fortunately (UNFORTUNATELY?), this is the one and only time this will happen because they note in my chart that I need to be tied into the wheelchair.

Now that I am cleared for a wheelchair and somewhat mobile, much like an adolescent discovering his newly found independence, I rebel. I have been denied so much for so long that I no longer care what is good for me, I just want what I want.

What I crave is water, lots of water. Because of my burns, strict limits are set on my daily intake of water. It appears that my sodium level is the benchmark for all decisions made regarding my care right now. Regardless, I am thirsty and want water. So early this morning, the adolescent in me takes a cup from my breakfast tray and hides it in my bed sheet. Now in my chair, I quickly wheel out of my room and head down the hall.

I furtively look over my shoulder and stealthily slip into the visitor's room. Inside this room, I know there is a water dispenser. Alone, I am finally able to slake my burning thirst as I drink cup after cup of water. I sit smiling, knowing that something so bad for me can also be so good. This rebellious act makes me feel just a little bit more human again.

The fun ends when the staff hunts me down and brings me back to my room.

There seems to be no serious ill effects of my foray to the visitor's room. It makes me wonder just how important it is that I am under such extreme fluid restrictions.

After settling into my routine at Parkland, I am a bit taken aback when I am told more surgery is necessary. They first must repair an aortic aneurysm. My aorta, the large artery exiting the heart which provides oxygenated blood to the body, is enlarged to greater than 1.5 times its normal size. The danger is that it might rupture and kill me. More surgery is also performed on my left leg in further attempts to save it. The doctors also tell me they will remove the small finger of my right hand. With only four fingers, I will now look like one of the cartoon characters from *The Simpsons*.

CHAPTER 3:
Fort Worth
March 1999 to August 1999

Ah, the day finally arrives: I am transferred from Parkland Hospital to Health South rehabilitation hospital in Fort Worth. I am reaching the point where I can be more independent and am actually feeling great, all things considered. The first thing I realize is that I will be away from the many restrictions placed on me while at Parkland. The second thing that makes me smile is that it will be far easier for my family and friends to visit me in Fort Worth than in Dallas. I am more conscious now, but my awareness of time and time passing is still clouded.

I believe I am finally done with surgeries and burn care. I surmise I will begin learning to live and move with only one leg and building my strength. I am still battling MRSA and Pseudomonas, though.

My things are gathered at Parkland and I am transferred by ambulance to Health South. I arrive in the evening and meet Dee who is the TBI director and the supervisor on duty. After she welcomes me, I panic as I discover that my picture of my son Kyle was left behind. I immediately start protesting and complaining. I want that picture returned and I want it *NOW!* Dee assures me she will contact Parkland and have the picture sent to my new quarters.

I am taken to a bed in the locked TBI ward. I protest loudly about being in this locked ward but am told that it is for my own safety because of my traumatic brain injury.

I am first visited by my parents and then by Tony and Jen. I find I am able to get into a wheelchair and move around the ward to socialize with other patients.

The next morning an admissions nurse asks me a series of somewhat standard questions. "Do you smoke?" "Do you do illicit drugs?" "Do you drink alcohol?" But then she blindsides me with the next question: "Have you had sexual relations recently?"

"Lady; seriously? I've been in the Parkland hospital burn unit for the last seven months. When and how would I have had sex?" I laugh.

She shrugs her shoulders and says "It is a standard question," and moves on to the next.

The question about sex does make me briefly think about sex again. Then reality hits me. "Who will want me now?" Sex is probably the least of my hopes and concerns.

After multiple protests, they finally agree to put me on a regular floor and in a regular patient room. After settling in, a therapist enters my room to review their schedule with me; these will be the visits from both physical and occupational therapy. I quickly interject, "I would like all of my sessions in the morning, with my afternoons and evenings left free to myself."

I'm sure the therapist is laughing under her breath before saying, "Mr. Norcott, if only that were possible. Mr. Norcott, you will be having therapy sessions both in the morning and in the afternoon. Our goal is to make you independent again and send you home. This isn't going to happen if you refuse treatment."

Her reply subdues me significantly because, more than anything, I do want to go home.

In the evening I get my first meal. Oh, mercy me! It is heaven! It is real food, not the nasty stuff I was fed at Parkland. Not only does this help strengthen my body, it also helps strengthen my spirit and I start feeling alive again!

The next morning, I begin realizing how different things will be here at the rehab hospital. At Parkland, everything was done for me, from transferring me in and out of bed, to bathing me and even wiping my behind. Now I begin doing all these things myself. The best part is there are no Penguin Squads dropping in on me and I am finally allowed to wear a gown so I am not naked all of the time. I have no real modesty left, but it is still nice not being constantly on display.

After breakfast my parents arrive with some of my own clothes. Once again, it is a very small step toward normalcy and my confidence continues growing.

A few days later, they remove the old dressing, examine my left leg, and tell me the infection and the grafts on my left leg are not healing properly. They give me terrible news, "Mr. Norcott, we must send you back to the hospital for evaluation. Your leg is not healing properly." This makes me most unhappy since I am reveling in freedoms I am enjoying here at Health South.

An ambulance awaits me and I am transported to Plaza Medical Hospital in Fort Worth. Once I arrive, I am met by three doctors: a plastic surgeon, an infection control doctor, and an orthopedic surgeon.

The recommendation of the plastic surgeon is to have a rod permanently inserted into my left leg and through the knee. This will completely immobilize my leg, causing me to walk like a pirate. The orthopedic surgeon tells me it is best if they amputate my left leg as well. He says it will be easier for me to adapt if both legs are gone.

Well, this is clearly not the news I want to hear, especially after having endured forty surgeries in various attempts to save this leg. I

THE TRAGIC & INSPIRATIONAL LIFE OF J. DAVID NORCOTT, JR.

do recall the few times at the rehab hospital when I went out with my dad. I recall the difficulties of getting around with only one leg. So, maybe the doctor is correct, maybe this is the best plan of action. It is April 1999, I am still heavily medicated, but I agree to their plan and both I and my parents sign the authorization allowing them to amputate my left leg.

Awaking the next morning, I notice that the dressing on my left leg is unusually large. I ask the doctor about this and He tells me that because of the infection they did not close the wound. The wound was left open and allowed to drain.

As if not enough has happened to me, I start noticing an itchy, painful discomfort all over my body. Even the hair on my arms seems to hurt and I have a temperature of 103. I learn that I now have diabetes. This happened because of my failure to thrive since the accident, which led to severe weight loss which was treated by a Total Parenteral Nutrition (TPN) diet (high fat and high calorie, given via a picc line) for too long. Because of the diabetes, the staff must now regularly check my blood sugar level. If too high, I am given a shot of insulin. It all becomes much too much and I begin protesting. What used to be merely annoying is now more pain than I can tolerate. I tell the nurses, "No more! You can do the blood glucose test and the insulin shots, but nothing else!"

My frustration and lack of cooperation does not sit well with my plastic surgeon. He comes in this morning, full of himself, yelling and threatening to put me into a nursing home unless I become more cooperative.

I shout back at him, "I am not about to agree to a nursing home. You need to first go and talk to my father! Now, get the hell out of my room!" With that I pick up the phone next to my bed and attempt throwing it at him. The phone is tethered to the wall so my dramatic moment falls flat as the phone drops abruptly onto my bed on top of me. The effect is not as I had hoped, but it felt good!

After what seems to be a rather short conversation with my strong-willed father, the same doctor, but with a very different attitude, re-enters my room. It is as if he is a new man. He is now quite calm and very polite. I knew my father would put him in his place.

The doctor tells me "Mr. Norcott, I understand your discomfort, but we really need to draw several blood cultures to determine the correct course of treatment for your multiple infections." Since he is now asking nicely, I suck it up and agree to the blood tests. The blood is drawn and the course of action is determined. Shortly thereafter the new antibiotic protocol is added to my IV. I begin feeling relief almost immediately.

The blood cultures reveal I have a systemic yeast infection and it is the source of the discomfort on my skin. So, I have yet one more infection and must face yet one more treatment. My dream of going home becomes more and more distant.

As I begin accepting my situation, I now start asking myself the question I have been avoiding. "Who is David Norcott?" With that question I also wonder these five points: "Who wants a man with no legs, no job, no car, no house and no money?" These questions will likely continue ringing in my head as my life progresses and I begin realizing I will probably be alone the rest of my life.

While I ponder dating, my poor parents are reaching their maximum in stress. At this same time, my sister enters a different local hospital to give birth to her second child. My mother and my father alternate staying with me and then my sister so that one of them is with one of us at all times.

Once again, the moment things seem to reach a near normal state, yet another problem arises. Now, shortly after I eat, I vomit. This is later followed by diarrhea. Because of this, I resist eating and I lose even more weight. Before the accident, with my legs, I weighed about 205 pounds. Now I weigh just above 100 pounds. Obviously not having my legs is part of the weight loss, but my torso is far thinner than before. The staff is concerned about my weight, but the food at here at Plaza Medical Hospital is no better than the food at Parkland. I pursue other options in food and discover there is a small hospital café with alternate foods. I find I can eat tuna salad, chicken salad, tapioca pudding and various flavors of *Jell-O*. This becomes my total diet. Not the greatest or healthiest of options, but at least I am able to eat and not continuously vomit.

Changing the dressing on my stump is a nightmare. Since the soft tissue often grows into the gauze of the bandages, the process is extremely painful. As the nurse slowly and gingerly attempts removing the dressing, the plastic surgeon becomes impatient, reaches over and quickly rips it off. I shriek in pain, a pain more intense than anything I have ever experienced in my life. I grip the arm of the nurse beside me so hard that it leaves a dark bruise on his skin.

This morning the nurses and therapists come into my room and tell me it is time I start spending more time in a chair and less time in bed. They assist in transferring me from one to the other. "Mr. Norcott, today we want you to sit in the chair for one hour. As the days progress this time will be lengthened." The next day I am given the most wonderful treat ever, I am taken outside on to a verandah. Overlooking the city, I enjoy breathing the sweet fresh air and feeling the warm sunlight on my face. I feel human again. I cannot help but think of movies from the 1940s and 1950s where hospital patients were shown regularly being taken outside to sit in the sunlight. It truly is the most restorative thing a hospital can do for a patient.

They finally take me to an Operating room to close and suture my left leg stump. This event signals the end of this hospital stay and tells me that I will soon return to the rehab facility at Health South.

After returning to Health South, my training continues with both physical and occupational therapy. One of my first lessons is making a bed. I am wheeled into a mock bedroom for this training. The therapist strips the bed of its blankets and sheets, leaving them in a heap. She tells me to make the bed. After much time, wheeling back and forth, I succeed! The bed is made and I pass this first test.

A few days later I experience chest pains. They are so intense that I suspect a heart attack. I alert the staff and undergo several tests. The tests indicate that nothing has happened or is wrong with my heart. In spite of the results, I am left with an uneasy feeling that something else is wrong, even though it may not be my heart.

My mother comes to visit and tells me that my maternal grandmother is in the hospital on life support. Her advance directive requires that all living children meet to decide the next step. My mother, ever the drama queen, pleads with me to go with her to Maryland. I look at her rather incredulously, wondering how she thinks I can possibly travel, but I feel a duty to my mother, my grandmother and also my father.

I ask the staff if can accompany my mother to Maryland. They are understandably hesitant and say, "We will call the prosthetics representative and ask what types of precautions should be taken for you to make this trip." The representative is also unenthused about my proposal but relents by saying, "If this is something you feel you really must do, at least let us put temporary covers over your stumps." The stump covers are put in place and along with my trusty wheel chair, I cautiously leave the hospital to join my mother on a flight to Maryland.

The trip goes well and is surprisingly uneventful, my grandmother is buried and her estate is settled. We fly back to Texas and are met at the airport by my father and sister.

On the way home we stop for lunch at one of my favorite diners, The Westside Café. Everything is fine until we arrive back at home. Once inside, I begin projectile vomiting. It is not food coming out, it is mucus. From my time as a paramedic, I know this is an indication of a gall bladder/pancreatitis issue.

My father immediately takes me to the hospital emergency room. They perform a sonogram, find nothing that concerns them and they send me home. I spend the night at my parent's house, but in the morning, the same scenario replays itself with more vomiting of mucus. Again, we go back to the emergency room. I have been out of the hospital and on my own just a little too long. I am no longer a docile, agreeable patient. I am now that horrible, problem person you see in movies. I fight with the staff over each thing they try to do for me, even though I know it is necessary and reasonable. The nursing staff is frustrated with my behavior and they finally consult a doctor. They return with a syringe and a smile on their faces. The contents of the syringe are injected into my IV and I slip off into a deep sleep.

The next thing I know, I am waking. I realize I am in a room in the Intensive Care Unit (ICU). I ask my nurse what has happened and she tells me to wait for the doctor and he will explain everything. The doctor enters and tells me they have removed my gall bladder. Instead of it being through several small incisions in my abdomen (the new way) it was done old style, with an incision from one side of my belly to the other. The surgeon tells me that my gall bladder, which is usually the size of a man's thumb, was more the size of a golf ball. Within my gall bladder was a gall stone so large that it filled the entire bladder.

The likely cause of the gall bladder problem is from the trauma of the accident and from the multiple resuscitations I received. Not surprisingly, it is called a traumatic gall bladder.

When finally discharged from the hospital there are problems re-admitting me to the rehab facility, so instead I head home with my parents. It makes me both happy and sad. As nice as it is for me, it puts additional pressure on my parents as I don't have the unique support I sometimes require, the kind the rehab facility can provide.

First of all, my stitches are still in place on my left stump. As the skin grows around the stitches, it becomes quite uncomfortable. The stitches really need to be removed but no one is here to take on this task and it doesn't really warrant a trip to the emergency room. I want them removed but it is clearly not something either of my parents is willing to do. The discomfort becomes so great I can no longer stand it, so, "David the Paramedic" decides to take things into his own hands.

I ask my father to retrieve a wound care kit along with alcohol. I know the kit will contain both tweezers and scissors. I get myself comfortable in bed and begin removing my own sutures. Watching nearby, my father is so tense that he appears to stop breathing. It is a surprisingly quick and painless process to remove them and it provides me with tremendous relief. As I remove the final stitch, I hear my father take in a long, deep breath.

A few days later I return to the rehab facility and continue gaining new freedoms. The facility encourages me to go on outings with my friends and family. When leaving the facility and especially getting in and out of cars, I do find that life is easier as a bilateral amputee (with no legs) than as before with one leg and one stump. I feel relieved that I made the right decision on that surgery.

The other thing I am learning is gratitude for my friends. Tony has been beside me since sixth grade and this tragedy has changed nothing. He is a rock and his wife Jen is a sweetheart. One night, Tony picks me up at the rehab hospital and takes me to dinner. Once in the restaurant, I fully realize my limitations. I need to pee, but I cannot navigate the restaurant in my wheelchair. Unlike at the rehab facility where I have options, here I am somewhat limited. I finally swallow my pride and tell Tony my dilemma. Tony doesn't even hesitate. He stands up and wheels me as close to the restroom as possible. He stops, walks around the chair, leans down and picks me up. Down the hall we go to the men's room. Once inside, he takes me into a stall and places me on the toilet. I don't have time to even feel embarrassed or awkward. Tony never reveals his own fears or concerns; he simply does what is necessary and needed by a friend. In my situation, it is good to have a friend who is an EMT, someone who isn't overly squeamish about such things.

Yes, Tony is an amazing man.

It is through these acts of kindness on the part of the medical staff, my family, and my friends that I finally begin seeing life from a different perspective. Life isn't just about me and my wants and desires. I am slowly learning gratitude. God continues molding me.

CHAPTER 4:
Home

This morning I awake to the most wonderful news imaginable. "Mr. Norcott, we are discharging you, sending you home." Wow, Home…. Looking up at a calendar, I realize it has been almost one year since my accident. Although I have been home a time or two, for the most part, I have been in the care of one hospital facility or another. But this is finally the end of this chapter, I hope.

While I was in the hospital, the management of my parent's apartment complex offered them another apartment. It was a beautiful spot, at the top of a hill. As lovely as it was for them, it is unworkable for me. The complex management tallied the costs of making access to the apartment easier for me and were shocked to find it would be about $8,000. Instead, they offered to move my parents and sister, at their cost, to a unit on a flatter part of the complex. There they could easily install a ramp, and so forth, to better aid my entry and exit. Upon arriving home, I discover that the new apartment is quite functional for me: I have access to all needed rooms, and I can easily use the bathroom, the kitchen, the bedroom, and the closet.

In spite of the challenges it presents, it is wonderful being home. As I grow more confident, I am also growing overly confident, even a bit arrogant: I am not being as careful as I should. The traumatic brain injury (TBI) and my lack of impulse control contribute to my reverting back to the old David, "I can do it! I'm ok! I'm tough!" But I'm not tough. I am more delicate than I care to admit.

Two weeks after coming home, I am finishing my business on the toilet. As I swing my stumps to the side to "dismount" I bump my left stump on the rail around the toilet and it begins bleeding. I inform my father of what has happened and he wants to take me to the hospital immediately. I, on the other hand, really do not want to return. I like being home. My father insists and I continue pushing back. I finally agree to call the doctor's office and let them decide. The office tells me to come in as soon as possible.

I sit waiting in the doctor's office with great trepidation. I am convinced everything is ok but I fear I will be sent back to the hospital, "just to be safe." I really do not want to return. I want to go home.

The doctor enters the examination room and listens to my story. He does a brief examination of my stump and reaches for one of those long Q-Tip-like sticks often used for a throat culture. I watch in near shock as he takes this stick and inserts it deep into my stump. I look up at my father and see that he is nearly white, the blood having drained from his face. As I worry that he may pass out, it suddenly dawns on me that I am not experiencing any pain. I look up at the doctor and ask, "What is going on? Why doesn't that hurt?" He replies, "You have osteomyelitis, a bone infection, and you have developed a sinus tract. The infection in your bone marrow is coming out. I'm sorry, Mr. Norcott, you *must* return to the hospital."

This time I head to John Peter Smith (JPS) hospital in Fort Worth. "Unhappy" doesn't properly describe my feelings. I am very upset and frustrated. After being examined by the ER doctor, I am sent to nuclear medicine for a scan of my stump. The scan is performed and I am taken to a room to await the results. As the clock ticks I feel the rage bubbling up inside of me. I look to the heavens and say to God, "I have endured quite enough. I simply want to go home and start my life again. I do not want yet one more challenge, one more hill to climb. I want to go home! Do you hear me?"

Since John Peter Smith Hospital (JPS), like Parkland, is a teaching hospital, back come the Penguin Squads. This morning's squad includes an orthopedic doctor. I suppose he is trying to make bad news seem not-so-bad, but my fuse is short and his almost flippant attitude infuriates me. He looks at me and says, "Well, Mr. Norcott I guess we will have to remove your left leg up to the hip."

I cannot help but remember a quote my father often said to me, "Don't swim half-way out in a lake, think you can't make it to the other side, give up and swim back." I never really understood what it meant as a child, but now I see how far I have come and how giving up or turning back is foolish. Yet, I'm not ready to lose my leg either.

I explode at the doctor "NO! No way! You are *NOT* removing my leg! I don't want just a second opinion on this, I want a third, fourth, and fifth opinion!"

Several doctors are brought in and after much discussion, they decide upon yet another course of antibiotics. When the nurse tries to start the IV, they discover my veins are protesting their year-long abuse. They have become restricted and it is almost impossible to start the IV. But one must be in place to give my body the medication it needs to fight the infection.

They insert what is called a central line, also known as a central venous catheter. A small opening is made near my neck and an IV-type line is inserted from there to a point near my heart. The wound is closed and antibiotics are fed almost directly into my heart chamber where they are pumped to the rest of my body.

With this line in place, they thankfully allow me to return home, but also tell me that I must return to the hospital in two days. At that time, I will have the central line replaced with a Hickman catheter. This is a larger gauge catheter than the central line and therefore less likely to clot.

After the new line is in place, the hospital tells me a home-health nurse will be regularly visiting me to administer the antibiotic treatments and to teach me the difficult task of changing the dressing.

Back at home, the bad news continues. It is October of 1999 and I learn my divorce is almost concluded and that my presence is requested at the final court hearing. The hearing is in Maryland, not Texas. Of course, this cannot be easy; it has to be very difficult. What do I do? I cannot afford to fly there, and besides, I do not really even want to go. I want that chapter of my life closed and I want to move on. But, because of my concern for my son and daughter, I decide to put on my big boy pants (figuratively, of course) and I ask my mother if she will go with me on this trip.

We buy bus tickets, pack and prepare for the long ride ahead.

Once in Maryland we find a cheap motel and settle in. The next morning, we both get ready and head to the courthouse. When my name is called, the judge's, mouth drops open. She looks at me and says, "I can't get people within this very county to appear, and yet here you are. In spite of your own personal issues and in spite of the distance, here you sit in my court. I'm impressed, Mr. Norcott, very impressed."

I don't know if my being there bought me any points with the court, but at least my divorce is over.

My mother and I head to the bus station and sit back for the long, thirty-six-hour ride to Texas.

As happy as I am to be home and to have my divorce finalized, I cannot help but think of the quote, "No good deed goes unpunished."

From all of the sitting on this long trip, I now have a fissure, a crack in the skin, at the base of my tail bone. It is basically the beginning of a bed or pressure sore. I take a two-pronged approach to treating it. First, recalling medical advice I was given many years ago by my grandmother, I ask my father to go to the store and get me a box of cornstarch. After my bath, I liberally apply the cornstarch to the affected area. Then, I basically spend the next several days lying on my stomach so that no pressure is applied to my sit-upon. This approach, along with IV antibiotics, administered by the home-health nurse, work well and within a week, the problem is gone.

I begin settling into life at home with my father, mother, and sister. Oh, and my sister's two sons, Antonio (Tony) and the infant Thomas. Tony and I become very close. Tony doesn't see me as "legless," he simply sees me as Uncle David. We start having great times together, especially after I get my power chair. With my power chair, Tony and I are able to take the bus (public transportation) together and explore Fort Worth.

One day, while at the pool with Tony, my sister introduces me to our neighbor Lecia. As we talk, Lecia asks me if I would mind watching her two children at the pool when I am there with Tony. I am tickled to death that a woman seems to be flirting with me and quickly agree. It also feels good that someone trusts me and sees me as a whole person.

The weather becomes warmer in the spring of 2000 and I decide I don't want to merely sit by the side of the pool, I want to get into the pool water myself. This is a new experience for me as an amputee and I am not quite sure what to expect. After motoring out to the pool area, I jump in the water. Well, my body isn't in the needed condition to do such a thing. Everyone panics as they watch my body bobbing up and down in the water with my head submerged and my stumps sticking straight up.

I quickly learn I must hold my core straight and actively work at keeping upright. After I show I have mastered swimming, my sister lets me take Tony swimming. For a while she keeps a watchful eye on both of us. It does not take long, though, before she feels comfortable that I am in control of the situation and so she begins sneaking off to do other things.

In many ways my life is becoming more normal, but I also realize that my brain is not working the same as before. I have problems with impulse control, irrational behavior, spending money with no thought to tomorrow, I am not sleeping correctly, and I do not regularly take my meds as prescribed. My moods are either overly elevated or I am horribly depressed; I am also overly assertive. In fact, I'm not even physically taking care of myself as I should. My spatial reasoning is poor as I am not able to put things in proper order. The frontal lobe of the brain, mine being damaged, is the filter of impulses. I am often frustrated because I know when something is wrong yet I cannot figure out how to fix it.

Through my Traumatic Brain Injury (TBI) Support Group I meet a wonderful woman, "Lou" Newman. Lou has a daughter, Libbey, to whom she introduces me. At one point in her life, Libbey was diagnosed with bacterial spinal meningitis; this led to hydrocephalus (water on the brain) which then led to nerve damage. Because of this, Libbey lost both of her legs. Unlike me, though, her amputations were below-the-knee. This experience also left Libbey suffering from TBI. Libbey is currently in school learning to be a prosthetist, to help other amputees. These two similarities cause us to forge a strong friendship

After listening to me tell her about my struggles and frustrations, Libbey suggests I look into brain cognition therapy and she recommends the program at Easter Seals. It is interesting that it isn't my case manager or even the doctors at Health South who help me with this, it is this young girl.

In the Easter Seals program, I begin relearning pretty much everything. I am a child again and I now must re-learn how to be an adult.

In August, during my regular medical check-up, they discover a bone spur is growing on the femur of my left stump. A bone spur is a boney projection that usually grows where two bones meet. In my case, it is my body's natural response to the amputation. The main problem with having the spur is that it prevents me from comfortably wearing prosthetics. My doctor recommends I return to the hospital for a surgery to remove the spur.

Now that I'm feeling and doing well, I begin venturing out more. My friend and partner at MedStar, Matt Nicholson, often comes over, picks me up, and takes me out. As I get out more, I discover the anti-tip protectors on my wheelchair often prevent me from crossing thresholds in doorways. So, I turn them up so they will not be in the way, although doing this leaves me vulnerable to tipping over.

In August 2000, Matt picks me up for an evening out. When he drops me off, I enter the apartment and hit an ottoman with my wheelchair. With the anti-tip protectors turned up and useless, the wheelchair and I flip over backward. As I fall, I foolishly attempt to break the fall by putting out my arm. This causes me to break my forearm at the wrist. I break both the radius and ulna bones.

While having my wrist treated for the break, I become concerned this will cause the other doctors to cancel the bone revision surgery. Since these two are rather unrelated issues, they decide to proceed with the revision surgery. I go back to the hospital for yet another operation.

After the surgery, I return home. With the loss of the use of one arm, I am greatly limited in my mobility. An occupational therapist comes to the apartment and prescribes a "super pole." The pole, much like a stripper pole, runs from floor to ceiling and gives me better stability getting in and out of bed.

One day as we all sit by the pool, Lecia's eight-year-old daughter asks if she may borrow my telescope that evening. I talk to Lecia, turn back to the girl and say, "Sure, no problem." Then, out of the blue, she looks up at the two of us and says, "You two get along well together, you really should go on a date!"

Lecia and I awkwardly look at each other, unsure of what to say. Lecia finally breaks the ice by saying, "Well, what do you think?"

What do I think? "Um.... Yeah!"

We finally go to a movie together. It is the first time I have been in a theater, in a wheelchair and ON A DATE!

We go on several dates after that. The relationship grows because she basically answers the five questions revolving around "who would want me?" I am actually feeling more whole now than I did when I had my legs. I feel like a man again, I feel real, and a woman wants me.

Lecia also *treats* me as if I am whole. My having no legs seems not to bother her at all. Knowing that I may be uncomfortable initiating sex, she eventually takes the lead. "Wow" is about all I can say. Afterward, if I could skip, I would.

On a trip to my TBI meeting, I find a dog roaming the parking lot without a collar or leash. Everything is going so well in my life that I decide to rescue this dog. He is very affectionate and fills yet another need within me. My mother, on the other hand, does not really want the dog around. When I am not home, she lets the dog outside unsupervised. The neighbors complain to the management, but my mother, concerned only with herself, keeps doing it.

So, we receive an eviction notice from the office.

Now, forced to move, we must find something quickly. Surprisingly, we find an apartment across the street. It is not a very nice complex and the apartment is far too small for someone with my mobility needs. There is a big difference between the words accessible and functional. I can access the apartment as a person in a wheelchair, but functionally, it is very poorly designed.

For example, the kitchen is so small that I have to enter it from one direction if I want to cook, then leave, turn around, and re-enter if I need to access the refrigerator. The bathroom is so small I cannot close the door when using it.

In the summer of 2001, my sister's husband separates from the Marines and my sister leaves Texas to move to West Virginia where he is now living.

One morning as I am bathing, I notice something on my stump that looks like a spider bite. I finish my shower and see that the wound is open and weeping. This is on my left stump, the same leg in which I had the osteomyelitis and the revision surgery. As I begin cleaning the wound, the gauze I use catches on it and as I try to pull it free, it pulls out a leftover encapsulated stitch from the revision surgery that had not dissolved. There is no great cause for concern, just another interesting morning in the life of David Norcott.

Lecia works in healthcare and has experience with people in poor health, so it is comforting to have her around. As our relationship grows, I feel more and more confident. I finish my cognition therapy with marked improvement. I am still on all of my medications, though, and still feel very dependent upon them. I get Meals on Wheels part time and I still get some at-home health care, yet I still have many of my own internal emotional issues which need resolving.

One day while attending my Fort Worth amputee support group I have the privilege of meeting Dana Bowman. Dana is an Army veteran who was hurt in a sky diving accident that killed his jump partner and left Dana as a bi-lateral amputee. In spite of this, Dana re-enlisted in the military and finished his career as a Golden Knight Parachutist (this is an Army performance group much like the U.S. Navy Blue Angels).

As "Jenny" was my tough-love nurse at Parkland, Dana becomes a similar motivating force in my life regarding my prosthetics. More than merely giving advice, he jumps on my case about my slow progress. He strongly encourages me to change prosthetic companies and from this, I meet Mark Ashford, with Hanger Clinic, and he becomes my prosthetist.

While at Hanger, one day, I also meet Dima. Dima is a bi-lateral amputee, but unlike me, one of his amputations was above the knee and the other below. I am stunned as Dima quickly slides his prosthetic leg over his stump, stands up and walks. I struggle with my prosthetics and sometimes it takes me almost one hour to properly fit them and walk.

At first, I am quite frustrated as Hanger Clinic wants me to take a "step" backward by going from my prosthetic legs back to what are called Stubbies. Stubbies are usually the first prosthetic device to which bi-lateral, above-the-knee amputees are introduced. They allow me to walk on my stumps but without affording me any height. Stubbies help me learn to walk, regaining a center of gravity and increasing my confidence. If I fall, I don't fall far. My gait improves almost immediately. Over time, they introduce lighter prosthetic legs and I make great "strides" in re-learning how to walk.

As the weather cools in Texas, with autumn approaching, I decide to take my biggest risk since the accident. I propose marriage to Lecia. We do not set a date as we have a lot of thinking and planning to do first. There are still a lot of unanswered questions, but we decide to tackle them as they come.

As the weather turns cold, my mother decides she misses her grandchildren and convinces my father they should move back to the northeast. My first thought is, "What about me? What am I going to do now?"

It is pointless reasoning with my mother or even playing off of her sympathies. So, in January 2002, my parents begin making plans to move to West Virginia. In March 2002 they actually move.

My father's departure is quite emotional for both of us. He actually breaks down and cries while saying his goodbyes. As upset as I am, I am also grateful to once again see the human side of this usually gruff man.

Once out of the apartment, I fully see what a mess it is. Lecia and her children come over to help. Both of my parent's smoke and the walls are horribly discolored; I also notice the smell coming out of the heat vent is that of an ashtray. I am so repulsed by the smell of stale smoke that I decide I will never smoke in this or any other home I ever occupy, nor will I permit anyone else to do so.

We finally get the place back to a livable state and I continue growing closer to Lecia. I know I made the right decision in asking her to marry me.

I am once again living on my own, having the support of Lecia and her children, but I continue having my own mountains to climb. I am still a bit hurt that my parents left me, but the cognition therapy has helped immensely and I begin working things out and continuing with my life.

Not wanting to make the same mistakes I made in my first marriage, I want my relationship with Lecia to be God centered. Lecia and I begin attending a church near our home.

As Lecia's birthday approaches, I think I can strengthen that objective by buying her a beautiful Bible and having her name imprinted on the cover. She is thrilled with the gift and the thought behind it.

Through a program by the Texas Rehabilitation commission, I start school at the local community college in computer repair. If any move in my life is ill-timed, it is this. As I am learning about it, the prices of computers plummet making them too expensive to repair, it is cheaper and easier to simply buy a new computer.

Lecia and I continue attending church regularly and our relationship thrives. We find a church that suits both of us and we ask to be baptized into that church. The church's new property was a horse arena for both training and performances and comes with the expected soft dirt, mud and fecal matter. Our Baptism is to be held in an antiquated barn with an old horse trough as the Baptismal pool.

Lecia goes first. As I await my Baptism, my rebirth, I marvel at how far I have come and how amazingly God has blessed me. In spite of my accident and my physical limitations, I am able to care for myself and I have a woman who loves me, a woman with whom I am starting a new life. This Baptism seems to be that logical and joyful next step.

My name is called. Wearing my stubbies I approach the Baptismal trough and get in. I am submerged into the water by the minister as he recites the ritual. At first, I think everything is wonderful.

As I exit the trough, I realize something is wrong. Instead of the Holy Spirit giving me a light yoke and an easy burden, I feel weighed down. I am quite uncomfortable and question what I have just done. Did I do something wrong? Did I say the wrong words? Is God rejecting me? Unable to process or understand what has just happened, my impulse is to go back to the trough and ask the minister to try again.

The reality is far less dramatic or spiritual. At this point in my recovery, added ounces to my weight feel like added pounds. The water from the trough got into both my prosthetics and the "feet" on them.

I go home, disassemble everything and let it all dry out. By morning, I am again David, son of God.

I continue growing in my independence and confidence. Two years ago, I would not even allow myself to dream that I could be where I am now. Yet, here I am. I am living alone, caring for myself and I have a woman who loves me and we are engaged to be married.

In the new year, 2003, I decide to take the next step. Since Lecia and her kids spend so much time at my place, I suggest we find a new place and all move in together. In this way we can save some money in preparation for our wedding.

About this time, Lecia's ex-husband, father of her children, loses his full-time job. This puts a strain on our relationship because he cuts off the child support to Lecia. I encourage Lecia to take him to court, forcing him to make the payments. Lecia refuses and I am too emotionally weak to insist she do so.

Once living together, we begin talking more earnestly about our wedding. After much discussion, we decide on August 9, 2003.

I continue working with Mark at Hanger Clinic and moving toward more functional prosthetic legs. They recommend Otto Bock brand computer knees, also referred to as C-Legs. The "C" stands for computer as there is actually a small microprocessor contained within each knee. These legs will allow me to walk step-over-step for the first time since the accident. I am excited and overwhelmed until I am told the reality of these new legs. They are expensive, very expensive, the co-pay alone is $20,000.

Is this a joke? Where can I get this kind of money? I can barely meet my monthly expenses!

As good as everything has been going, this crashes me back to reality. I allow myself to wallow in self-pity for a while, and then I pull myself up and begin considering my options. I decide to first approach the Texas Rehabilitation Commission (TRC) for advice. They offer financial help as well as suggesting other options for fundraising. While my case manager at TRC contacts the United Way, I contact Limbs for Life. I fill out their paperwork explaining how these new prosthetic legs will help me and they take photographs of me for the file.

Incredibly, at this same time, a reporter with The Fort Worth Star Telegram newspaper comes out to interview those of us in the Fort Worth Amputee Support Group at Harris Hospital. I am interviewed and amazingly, my story and my seeking money for the prosthetics co-pay is a large part of the story.

Gary Oliver, the bishop at Benbrook Tabernacle of Praise, where I attend, happens to read this article. I am a rather quiet and subdued person within my church and am very surprised Sunday morning when the minister begins talking about me. He quotes the article in the newspaper and asks the congregation to dig deeply into their pockets and wallets to help me. The collection plate is passed around specifically for me that day. All totaled, I receive a little over $3,500 toward my goal. I am overwhelmed and relieved at the same time. In spite of my joy, this also sets up a small conflict inside of me as to how I can contribute or give back to those who have been so wonderful to me.

So, between my church, the United Way, Limbs for Life, and the Texas Rehabilitation Commission (TRC), I now have enough to cover the co-pay for my new C-Legs.

With everything in place, I am more excited and anxious than ever to receive my new prosthetic c-legs. My wedding is weeks away and I want more than anything to be standing as I wed my angel Lecia. My prosthetist, Mark, cautions me that something could easily go wrong.

He states, "Don't worry, you *will* get your new legs, but know that a million things can delay their delivery. I want you to wear them at your wedding as well, but you might want to consider a Plan B."

About two weeks before my wedding, the clinic calls with the best news ever! "Mr. Norcott, your new prosthetic legs are ready. When can you come in for the first fitting and trial?"

I am so elated that I can probably leap there on my stubbies alone.

At the clinic, I slip easily into the sockets of the new legs, stand up quickly and take my first steps. I am using two canes, but it is still an amazing feeling. I am walking again!

So, how do I feel? Like I just won the lottery; it is like standing in utopia. For the first time in my life, I feel like Joseph David Norcott, Jr. I see who I truly am rather than someone else's idea of who I should be.

Here is this incredible, amazing moment and suddenly the old David with all of his "not worthy-ness" appears. I suddenly withdraw into my childhood comfort zone. "David, you aren't worthy of all of this. Think of all of the people who helped you, of the money they donated, think of the people who need this gift more than you. David, you are nothing; nobody. How could you let all of this happen?"

In spite of all of the obvious affirmations, all of the generosity, all of everyone's hard work, I am still incapable of simply feeling gratitude. As much as the outer, physical David is being repaired, the inner David is still quite broken.

I continue volunteering at UpReach, Inc., the school where I went for computer technician training. I do a variety of odd jobs, such as answering the phones, responding to e-mail, etc. While in the office, I begin walking around without my canes, gaining confidence. Of course, just when I think I have the hang of it, I trip and fall. I repeat the same prior, foolish mistake with the same arm as before, I push out with my hand to break the fall, which causes a small chip fracture in the ulna bone of my wrist. With my wedding and honeymoon around the corner, I don't dare go and see a doctor. Instead Lecia and I go to the drug store and I buy a Velcro wrist brace. It helps only slightly, and so I am forced to simply endure the pain.

The wedding is in our house. We invited over 200 people and expect about 100 to actually attend. I am so happy, so pleased and so proud as I stand here on my own new legs, in front of my friends and family, watching my beautiful bride come down the aisle toward me.

It is a glorious day. Everything seems perfect. I reflect at how much my life has changed and how far I have come. I think, "Nothing can be better!"

We spend the night in our home. Tomorrow we leave on our honeymoon and officially start our marriage. Our honeymoon isn't a strictly traditional affair. Lecia's parents, and her aunt and uncle, go with us. Lecia's parents are nice enough to let us use a portion of their timeshare condo in Branson, Missouri. Since this is their special holiday getaway place, they come along as well. Another reason they join us is because Lecia's father brings my power chair on the back of his truck. We are quite the convoy heading north through Texas to Missouri.

Our stay in Branson starts on a very high note as we are all quite excited to be here. We decide to take in a few shows and also plan to visit the amusement parks.

The second day for me is very special. It is my first trip to an amusement park since the accident and I declare to everyone that I want to ride the roller coaster. I suspect my family is a little unsure of this, but we get into the line and wait our turn. It is a "stand up" roller coaster and I am on my new legs. WOOOSH – off we go! The emotional thrill of me being on that ride is almost more than I can stand. My smile extends from California to Florida, with a brief stop in Branson. As we pull back into the boarding area, everyone can see how elated I am. I can't stop smiling and thoughtlessly say, "Can I go again?" I know there is a line of people waiting, but it just slips out. The operator looks and me, smiles and says, "You bet!! Enjoy yourself!" The reality of what I am doing hits me. I look over at the crowd and say, "Well, there are others waiting…" The crowd looks at me and yells, "GO AGAIN!" I go three times in a row.

It isn't just the thrill of the ride; it is mostly that I am able to ride and enjoy it as a "normal" person. Between my wedding and this trip, I feel like a whole man again. After a full day in the park, we return to the condo for a relaxing evening and good night's sleep.

The next day we go to a different amusement park. We are approaching the gates when I am triggered. While paying, the attendant looks me up and down and says, "No charge."

"What? Why not? Do you think I cannot ride the rides?" I go from being on top of the world to falling back into my pit of despair and victimhood. "Who do you think you are?" This is the reality of a PTSD Storm and a TBI Trigger. What would seem to be a non-event causes a severe emotional reaction in me.

I become pissy and nasty. Lecia notices my dramatic mood change and tries talking to me. I'm so angry I cannot give her a coherent answer. I'm having what I call a "silent tantrum." I'm mad, I want everyone to know I'm mad, but I don't really want to do anything about it. I just want to be mad. Of course, the end result is that I'm ruining everyone else's good time.

The reality is that even though I now have my legs, I still have major emotional problems. My primary causes are PTSD and my TBI, also, I have never really dealt with my issues from childhood. I've been too busy trying to help and fix others and have not worked on healing my inner self. I also have not yet fully accepted that no matter how good things might be, they will never be totally the same as before.

One thing is for sure, when things don't go my way, I am excellent at being a raging lunatic. Tantrum is too mellow a word to describe the volcano inside of me and it is a volcano that is always on the edge of erupting.

CHAPTER 5:
David Before David

So, how did I get here? How did all of this happen? Who exactly *is* Joseph David Norcott, Junior?

I guess the best place to start is at the beginning. I was born in New Jersey in 1967. I was an only child until I was nine years old when my sister, Holly, was born.

My father was in the Army at the time of my birth. His life was one of rules and discipline, a life that rarely included love and tenderness.

My father was born in New York City but raised in Miracle Hill Ministries, an institutional boy's home in South Carolina. A place such as that is not a place to experience much of anything other than strict rules paired with harsh punishment for breaking those rules. But my father was a survivor and he made it through the system.

Somewhat understandably, he drifted into the military; it was a structure with which he was familiar and within which he was comfortable.

Sadly, these experiences did not lend themselves to being a loving or doting father. Joseph Senior did what he knew best: he set rules and he doled out harsh punishment for breaking those rules. I was regularly both verbally and physically abused under the guise of discipline.

This left me emotionally empty. I was also terribly confused as these rules seemed to apply only to me, never to my father or my mother. Because of this, I often rebelled and became even more the son my father was convinced could be "tamed" by greater and greater amounts of corporal discipline.

My mother, on the other hand, was concerned only with herself. She had been raised as a victim and victimhood was the badge she displayed at all times. As is the trait of victimhood, she never took responsibility for anything in her life. Everything was always someone else's fault. Along with this, my mother was an alcoholic. She was also not above her own abusive qualities, and I was often the target of her frustration, anger, and her emotional vacuum. She cared only about having her needs satisfied while doing her best to avoid my father's anger.

I also had to witness the regular nightmare of my father's physical abuse against my mother.

This put me on a path where I became a horrific mix of all of their negative qualities. As much as I disdained them, I became them.

As I grew older, I too only cared about my own physical and emotional needs. Oddly, I developed a fascination with careers that involved helping others. The outer David wanted only his personal needs met, but the inner, secret, David wanted to help others. This dichotomy seems to be the blending of my true inner passion and desire melded with a healthy dose of my childhood circumstances and abuse.

In my early teens, I was enthralled by the television series *Emergency*, about the exploits of Johnny Gage and his partner Roy DeSoto, both firefighter paramedics with the Los Angeles Fire Department. I watched in awe and knew that I wanted to be a firefighter paramedic as well.

My dreams of becoming a paramedic were further confirmed by the television series *M*A*S*H*. Watching these medical professionals help and heal others intrigued me and made me want to do the same.

In helping and healing others, I hope to heal myself. As a paramedic, I can only address the physical pain people experience. My pain is internal, it is emotional, it is my soul that needs healing. This is something only God can help me heal.

At the age of 15½, I enthusiastically joined the local volunteer fire department as a probationary junior volunteer. With that came a uniform. That uniform and I became one; it became my identity. In many ways it was also my temporary salvation.

As I matured, I continued learning about emergency medicine and did everything necessary to become a certified emergency medical technician (EMT). At the age of 17, I received that certification, allowing me to ride with other EMTs. While in school and training, I also found satisfaction by helping a man who was a quadriplegic. He lived in a nursing home where my mother briefly worked. I would help bathe, dress and feed Bobby O'Kelly. When necessary, I would drive him around town to various appointments. It is interesting to me that I so closely helped and bonded with a man who in many ways represented what I was to become.

Maybe because of the help I provided him, it allowed me in my time of trouble to accept help.

In spite of these seemingly kind acts, I still lived life doing just barely what was necessary to get by. I wasn't a "fine young man." I was consumed with my own wants and needs. This was especially apparent in my romantic alliances. All I wanted was to date and have sex. I did not and could not open myself to a true loving and caring relationship.

At age eighteen, I received my Officer in Charge status. As was true for my father in the Army, I easily adapted to life in the Fire Department where the rules were clearly posted. I knew what was expected of me, yet, at the same time, those rules triggered my need to rebel. If I was not rebelling against the rules, I was rebelling against life.

When I turned 25, I married my girlfriend and we began establishing a life for ourselves. I, of course, was not prepared for this. I did not know how to be a good husband and I definitely did not know how to be a good father. I only knew how I was raised. In other words, our marriage was doomed from the very beginning.

The longer I was an EMT, the more it became my identity. I became so distant from my responsibilities and duties at home, that I would do everything to avoid being there. More than once as I drove from the station to my house, I would pull over and vomit as the stress of being a family man was far too much for me.

To avoid being at home, I would take more and longer shifts at work. I was a good paramedic but a terrible husband and father.

I was the type of man who wanted to win every battle, thinking that it would somehow lead to winning the war. It didn't matter which battle or which war – they all needed to be won. Of course, it was this same destructive mindset that led to the accident on September 3, 1998.

I thought I was taking care of my problems by taking care of others. Well, I was wrong about that too. Naturally, the less I was home, the less my wife needed or wanted me. This eventually led to her filing for divorce in July 1996.

As much as I struggled with my marriage, the divorce filing devastated me and I began a slow spiral downward. It was a battle I could not win and I realized that I could not heal myself by healing others. I wasn't "fixed," I was still badly damaged. I became extremely depressed and withdrawn.

Because of this my friend and brother paramedic, Tony Occhipinti, intervened. Tony decided to move to Texas and was not about to leave a pitiful, sad David behind. Tony encouraged me to move as well. He did just about everything but load the truck, throw me in the back with my stuff, and drive to Texas.

Upon arriving in Texas, we both applied at MedStar, were both interviewed on the same day, we were both hired, and we were both part of the same class in August of 1997.

PART II:
Night

*"Out of the depths
I cry to thee, O Lord!
Lord, hear my prayer!"
– Psalms 130:1*

*" Those who God loves most,
He allows to suffer most."* - Anonymous

CHAPTER 6:
Decline

Now in our home together, Lecia and I begin establishing ourselves and our lives. We quickly discover the things we *should* have talked about before marriage, but instead, like most couples, we are blithely indifferent, trusting love will conquer all. One of our first major problems centers around raising Lecia's daughter.

For the most part the problems concern her schooling and homework. Lecia and I have very different approaches and to stop the conflict, Lecia simply stops talking to me about it. She also withholds her daughter's report cards from me.

These are the beginning cracks in not only our relationship, but also in my sense that I have achieved a normal life and that I am now "whole." The reality is that I am still broken, still unable to handle relationships and responsibility. The more things between us fracture, the more I distance myself, just as I did in my first marriage. I am often angry and sullen. This, of course, solves nothing.

On my way to an appointment one day, I stop off at McDonalds for lunch. As I wheel my chair into the restaurant, I am stunned when I see Cecil Bacher, the paramedic who saved my life the night of the accident, standing near me. We exchange casual greetings, unsure of what to actually say to each other. The awkwardness between us suddenly changes when I have an overwhelming experience, a sense of peace, love, and joy. Suddenly tears are streaming down my cheeks and the same happens to Cecil. As I gather myself together, I wonder what is going through Cecil's mind as he sees me here. Seeing how damaged I appear, is he regretful that he put so much time and effort into saving me? Cecil knew me before the accident, now here I am legless and confined to a wheelchair. Does he feel guilt or joy in knowing that his efforts were successful?

Back home, I try to think of ways to save my troubled marriage. I decide that getting a dog might be a good idea. A dog would be the perfect thing for me and maybe in refocusing myself I can save my marriage. Of course, this is silly. I need to fix myself; I don't need diversions.

Regardless, I seem to be led to the Humane Society website. There I quickly find a Doberman named Beauty. I immediately know that I need to meet her and I call the Humane Society to set up an appointment.

CHAPTER 7:
Lady

I am told her name is Beauty. What I didn't know from the picture and description on the internet is that she has a problem with her right front leg. When the family and I go to meet her, she is in recovery from having that leg amputated. If ever there is or was a perfect dog for me, it seems to be Beauty. As they bring her out to meet us, my heart stops beating for a moment.

Here I am, a man with no legs looking at a dog who is missing one leg. I know immediately that I want this dog.

As they walk Beauty past me, she stops, looks at me and rests her chin on my thigh. I have to quickly pull myself together so I do not cry in front of everyone. Yes, this is my dog. I quickly say a silent prayer that both Lecia and the kids want her as well.

The kids go outside with her to play. Lecia can see the look on my face and knows I have to have her. After a short while, Beauty and the kids came back in with smiles on their faces and the kids needlessly plead with me that we adopt her.

I smile at the woman with the Humane Society and say, "Yes, we'll take her."

I fill out the necessary paperwork and begin the wait. We hit a couple of snags along the way, but we finally get the call and Beauty is now ours. Watching her in our home, she shows many signs of a delicate, elegant lady. On one hand, if it is raining, she will not go outside to do her business. She looks up at me as if saying, "Not today. Could someone else go for me?" On the other hand, if the weather is nice, the elegant lady in her becomes a great hunter as she boldly runs out and chases any squirrel in our yard. Despite missing her front leg, she is quick and often just clips the tail of the squirrel she pursues.

Because of her often delicate, lady-like behavior, we rename her "Lady." She and I have a similar soul and a similar story so we quickly bond. She loves the entire family, but there is no doubt to anyone that she is my dog.

As in every other step of this story, God must also have had a hand in my finding Lady. She is perfect for me. She helps calm the storms in my head and smooths out my often-turbulent emotions. With Lady's help, I pray I can hold together all of the good that has happened in my life including my marriage.

CHAPTER 8:

Victimhood

God's work has only just begun. Seeds have been planted, the new path should be obvious, but I still cannot seem to realize that I must first fix myself. I have not, as yet, sunk low enough. This attempt at rebuilding my life is failing. It is my fault; it is my problem. The gratitude I initially felt for those helping me to get my prosthetic legs has now devolved into an attitude of entitlement. The world now "owes" me. God presents me options and I consistently choose the wrong ones.

I find myself in a position I have never been in. I begin waffling between being grateful and being a victim. Hey – I'm an amputee, the world *owes* me! Don't people realize what I have been through?

As much as I thought I was grateful for the help I received paying for my c-legs, that gratitude is slipping into entitlement. It is the beginning of my slow slide into victimhood. Instead of approaching issues from the attitude of "what can I do? How can I make this happen?" I now expect others to accommodate me; in fact, I *expect* the entire world to accommodate me.

The world pushes back and says "No!"

Just as I retreated into my work as a paramedic in my first marriage, now I retreat into this state of victimhood when things do not go my way. The one thing I know for certain how to do, when things do not go my way, is to be an ass. This is my comfort zone.

Interestingly, Lecia takes the same path as I did in my first marriage. She begins working longer hours to avoid me and our mutual "mistake."

As if to mock me, the winter of 2003/2004 is one of violent, heavy storms and rain. The lakes and creeks rise and we awake one morning to a flooded home. In addition to the flooding, our power is out.

Our landlord does his best to repair and handle everything, but as 2004 marches forward, we grow tired of the constant repairs and the inconvenience of periodically having to live in motels.

Good times do not last long, though. My mother calls and informs me that she is returning to Texas to live with me. She has been living in a nursing home after living for a while with my sister. My sister grew tired of our mother living in her house and insisted she move into a care facility. I thought she was out of both of our lives, but it isn't so. I call my sister to find out what happened when mom was living with her. "She is just too disruptive. In spite of my best efforts, she crosses far too many lines. She is always creating chaos within my family. I could not take it any longer, so I moved her into a senior care facility."

Wonderful, now she will be my problem. I agree to take her for two reasons. First, out of sympathy for my sister, who has borne this burden for far too long and secondly, I hope she will be able to obey the few rules we place upon her. "Hope" is the operative word here.

In January 2005, we decide it might be best to look for another home. My dream has always been for us to own our own place and establish roots. I pray that somehow, this will make everything better. My fantasies and expectations want this to be true so I push forward.

I recall the shows on television where crews fix up a house for a worthy family. "Well, if ever there was someone who was worthy, it is me!" I selfishly think. "I deserve and am entitled to a 'special' home too." So begins my next trek, my next diversion from actually dealing with my own issues and problems. My newfound victimhood merely amplifies my own inner problems and demons. It solves nothing, yet I march forward in finding a way to get me and my family a new house that also meets my needs as an amputee.

Lecia and I are at Sam's Club picking up the usual necessities when I turn and see Cecil Bacher standing in the aisle. I am in a power scooter and I see a woman with Cecil also in a scooter. I introduce Cecil to my wife, Lecia, and Cecil introduces us to his mother. Pleasantries are exchanged all around. As happened earlier at McDonald's, there seems to be something silent, something unspoken, yet something that probably needs to be spoken between us. In spite of the silence, I still sense a deep, soulful appreciation. It is very much an agape experience for me.

In pondering ways for us to find a house that meets my special needs, we notice the name of one of the home builders on a television show and decide to call. We discover they are currently building a development in our area. Lecia and I go down and meet with the company to see what they can do for us.

We meet with the builder and I smugly lay out my demands for the special modifications necessary to the new home. After finishing and expecting them to simply roll over and accommodate me, they hit me with reality. "Yes, we can do all of that for you, once you secure funding. We cannot make those modifications unless we know for certain you will be buying the house. Once modified to meet your special needs, the house becomes almost impossible for us to sell to anyone other than you."

"Well, considering my situation, certainly there is a federal, state, county, and/or city program that will have to help me!" I selfishly think. Yes, the programs do exist, but the house must first meet the standard of *Catch-22* approval for such a program.

I'm now in the classic situation. The builder will not modify the house without the loan and the lender will not grant the loan without the house meeting its standards.

I go back to the builder, tail between my legs, and accept many concessions. I limit my demands to a few things I view as absolutely essential. Thankfully, the builder views these changes as generic enough that they can be done without making the house overly unique.

The house is completed in August 2005 and we joyfully move in. The modifications are not perfect but they do allow me certain freedoms I have not been able to enjoy in quite some time.

The new home is so large and well configured that my mother can basically have her own private "apartment" in our house. She has not only her own bedroom, but a separate living area as well. My mother brings with her the same chaos she brought to my sister's home and along with this chaos is her litany of excuses. As usual, nothing is *ever* her fault.

Hmmm… I'm beginning to see from whom I learned "victimhood."

Lecia is running out of patience. Not only does she try to go with me to all of my various medical appointments, she is raising her children and now is trying to make my mother happy. She does not fully understand that that last objective is unattainable. My mother is a steamroller of chaos and discontent. She thrives on it. My mother simply does not want to be happy; just as my natural state is anger, my mother's is misery. Our new common bond is that we are now both victims.

I am unhappy, Lecia is unhappy, and the kids are unhappy. In spite of this, we continue lumbering along, trying to remain a family.

My mother agreed to pay a small amount of rent when she first moved in, but each month the amount we receive gets smaller and smaller. There is always some sort of excuse.

Finally, on Thanksgiving 2005, we reach our breaking point. One of the only hard and fast rules I have with my mother is that there is no smoking in our new home. As Lecia and I lie in bed, her head suddenly pops up, she looks at me and says, "Do you smell that?" I pause, take a few sniffs and smell the cigarette smoke as well.

We get out of bed to investigate and find my mother smoking in her bed. Not only does this break our rules, it is also extremely dangerous because she is currently on oxygen. She is placing her life in jeopardy and she could easily burn down the entire house.

This is it. My mother has to go. I don't care where she goes, but she must leave my house.

The next morning, we call adult protective services to inquire about our options. This also prompts me to call both my sister and my father.

After much begging on my part to my father, he agrees that she can move back to Pennsylvania and live with him.

We take my mother to the airport and I actually wait to ensure she is aboard the plane. The flight leaves for Chicago where she will change planes and continue to Pittsburgh. During my mother's flight to Chicago, my father changes his mind, "No, I don't want her here, I don't care where she goes, but it won't be here."

My mother learns of my father's decision when she lands in Chicago. With the money she had saved by not paying us rent, she buys a ticket to West Virginia to see if she can guilt my sister into taking her back. This is a bad idea, really bad. My sister had enough of our mother months ago and has no intention of letting her back into her home.

Regardless, my mother arrives at the home of my sister and Holly flat out refuses to let her in. With nowhere else to go, my mother walks around the house to my sister's back patio and becomes a squatter.

My sister is furious but unsure of what to do. After several calls to me, she finally contacts a senior adult assistance office in her town. They aid in getting my mother into a senior care facility. Of course, the facility also has rules and, of course, my mother refuses to follow their rules too. They tell her they will expel her from the home, but she continues creating more chaos for everyone. Along with upsetting the staff, my sister and I now must field regular phone calls from her while she complains about everything.

Whether out of guilt or duty, I talk to my mother regularly. Each call brings the same litany of complaints and frustrations. She wants to be miserable and there is really nothing either my sister or I can do about it.

At the care facility, she discovers she is not required to go to the communal dining area to eat. She can request the staff deliver the meals to her room. This does not end her complaining, but it does stop the complaints by the other residents to the staff about her.

We all continue along with things as they are. Sad but stable.

CHAPTER 9:
Freefall

In early 2006, I again suffer my annual allergic reaction to certain elements in the Texas air. I am so miserable that I ask Lecia to take me to the emergency room. In the room, I am stunned when the attending nurse enters as it is Cecil Bacher! Again, we are both pleasantly surprised and he tells me that he got his Registered Nurse (RN) license and is now working here in the emergency room.

He has a job to perform, but a big part of me just wants him to sit down and talk with me. I have many unanswered questions about that night. I also would like to resolve that unknown I sense between us.

It is the spring of 2006. My life is being held together by kindergarten paste and prayer.

Our family gets a big surprise today. Lecia's youngest daughter, who is seventeen, announces that she is pregnant.

I am unhappily shocked that Lecia seems pleased, so I am terribly confused. I finally ask Lecia about this and she replies, "Well, at least she is older than I was when I first got pregnant."

I sit mutely because I don't know how to even respond to that.

With the announcement comes a dramatic shift in our marriage and in our family. Lecia begins ignoring me while pouring all of her love and attention into her pregnant daughter and future grandchild.

It is far beyond the normal excitement one might expect. I know she is trying to repair some of the hurt within herself from how her parents reacted when she made the same announcement to them. But this is out of hand.

She gives so much attention to this one daughter that even her other children and grandchildren begin noticing and they respond by rebelling. Although they are angry with their mother, they decide that I am somehow ultimately to blame for the situation. Now everyone is angry and ignoring me.

In spite of an earlier attempt to wean myself from all of the prescription drugs I have been taking, I am now taking more than ever before. It is a constant downward spiral and the iciness between Lecia and me grows.

Our marriage is doomed at this point and we both know it, but our lives are too intertwined to simply walk away. Instead, we continue on down this most uncomfortable and unhealthy path.

We are both clearly responsible, we are both unhappy, but neither of us wants to take the first necessary step.

As I become increasingly depressed, I rely heavily on my prescription medications to get me through the days. Like my mother, I withdraw and spend most of my time in the office room of the house where I sit surfing the internet. I spend a lot of time watching pornography and periodically enter chat rooms for some form of female connection and attention.

I believe, sensing the end of our marriage, Lecia's 24-year-old married son comes and asks her to co-sign a car loan. Surprisingly, Lecia discusses this with me. I remind her that with the house payment and other costs of our home and car, we cannot really handle any financial upset in our lives. So, I tell her I would rather she not do this.

In spite of my wishes, the two of them head out to shop. Now, should he find an older, used, less expensive car, I might be open to helping him. Of course, this is not the case; he finds a newer late-model car, believes he is getting a great deal and Lecia calls me, begging for my "permission."

Now I am angry that I am being put in this position. The depression and drugs do not help me think clearly, either. To simply make the problem go away, I agree. I know where this path is heading, but in spite of my clouded judgment, it appears the train will crash no matter what I do or say.

Amazingly, after the papers are signed and the car is driven home, Lecia's brother calls me. At one point he and I were fairly close, but as my relationship with Lecia unraveled, so did my friendship with him.

Her brother makes the most interesting comment, "It's a good thing you agreed to help my nephew because Lecia would have signed the papers anyway."

Wow, so I basically do not even exist in this marriage. I'm merely flotsam and jetsam.

Time passes and we continue living together, but on separate planes. We rarely talk or interact. In late 2007, December approaches and with it my fortieth birthday. I am in no mood to celebrate. I am about to turn forty and here I am with no legs, a wife who ignores me and no clear path to anything ever changing. The word "depressed" barely covers what I am feeling.

Lecia suddenly becomes quite interested in me and my upcoming birthday. She wants to throw me a party. I reluctantly agree and she surprises me with a wonderful novelty cake that she has made. It is the backside of a full-figured woman and she is wearing a G-string. Amongst the gifts are my favorite cigars and a small bottle of cognac. I sit back, light up a cigar and pour myself a glass of the cognac. Well, maybe forty isn't all that bad after all, I decide.

Our crippled marriage continues within its completely dysfunctional parameters. About this time, my conversations and e-mails to other women on the internet become more frequent and bolder. I have not personally met anyone, but my messages are clearly not platonic.

In August 2008, Lecia finds some of these e-mails and confronts me. I explain that they are messages only, but the damage is done.

One day Lecia helps me wrap my stumps. Afterward, I decide to take an afternoon nap. When I awake, the house seems unusually quiet. I get up and into my chair. Moving around the house I realize that no one is home and I assume they have all gone to the store.

I finally pick up my phone and look to see if I missed any calls while sleeping. There, on the phone, is the "Dear John" text message I have feared receiving. Lecia has left, taking with her the only car that is configured for me to drive. So here I am, stranded and all alone.

Now with no car and a newly found raging thirst for alcohol, I regularly take myself on my power chair to the nearest liquor store. I basically drink from breakfast until bedtime. I am so addicted that I never waste a single drop. Anything left in a glass is poured into an ice cube tray and frozen for my drink the next morning.

Lecia and I both experienced a lot of childhood trauma as well as adolescent trauma. I would like to point the finger of blame at her, but neither of us has ever really attempted to deal with our own pain and brokenness. I know how to get into a marriage, but I have never known how to make one last. I try counseling but cannot stay the course. In many ways we both marvel at how far we both have come and how much we have accomplished, but that alone does not fix the inner pain and the problems it creates. It is much like my desire to help others while being unable to help myself.

I finally talk to an attorney to explore my options. He tells me to proceed gingerly, not wanting to see things get completely out of control. He tasks me to protect my assets and I open a new personal bank account at a new bank. I figure this one step is enough for now.

I still hold out hope that our marriage can be saved, foolish as that may seem. Too much has happened to seriously consider reconciliation, but I really do not want yet another divorce for either of us.

Lecia learns of the new checking account and this begins the "if you did this then I'm going to do that!" phase of our breakup. Between my medications and the alcohol, I am just not interested anymore and have no fight left in me.

Surprisingly, Lecia does return. I am confused but try to assume the best. I prepare a separate room for her and our few days together are cold but civil.

I awake this morning, sober for once, and decide I've been trapped in the house for far too long. With Lecia here, my car is available for me to drive. I get everything together and head out on a day long road trip. I have no particular destination in mind, I'm just driving.

When I return at night, Lecia is not home. I awake the next morning, and the car and Lecia are gone.

So – it's over.

In October 2008, I find an apartment for myself and move out of the house. I decide to simply let the house slip into foreclosure.

Now I am really alone and on my own. I turn to the State for assistance, finding the programs for which I qualify. I realize what I really need is someone to help me during the week with many of the tasks previously handled by Lecia.

I respond to an ad on the internet from a young woman looking for work as an aide.

As if being addicted to my medications and alcohol is not enough, I decide to add marijuana to the toxic mix as well.

I interview Tina, the woman from the internet post. I give her the job and she helps me in many ways such as cooking, cleaning and shopping. Over time she begins also helping me by both satisfying my sexual needs and supplying me with marijuana. She basically becomes my whore and drug dealer.

It is a dysfunctional yet comfortable relationship, especially since the State is covering most of the costs. Once again, I sign up for Meals on Wheels and find I can just eke out my life while eating periodically, taking my prescription medication regularly, drinking often and smoking pot almost constantly. I'm deeply depressed and wildly over-medicated.

One day I meet my neighbors, Andrew and Glenda Bashor. They are absolutely the finest of people and despite me being broken and pathetic, they decide to help me. I learn that Andrew is a local-route truck driver. The two of them are model Christians and for whatever reason, they care about me.

In many ways, I know they shouldn't help me, that I really need to simply bottom out. One of the first things Andrew does to help me is to go with me to get my last few things out of the house before the foreclosure. In addition to my personal belongings, I also take the stove and the refrigerator for good measure.

I receive most of my disability money at the end of the month. So, at the beginning of each month I buy brand-name liquor and by the end of the month I buy any rot-gut brand I can still afford.

So now my life is one of self-pity, victimhood, alcohol, marijuana, pornography and sex with my aide. This pretty much defines me. I can't bother eating properly either. If it doesn't numb my pain, I am not really interested.

With all of the struggle and joy in getting my prosthetic legs, I now mostly wear them as decoration. It is just too easy to motor around in my power chair. I have no motivation and no reason to think anything is going to change in my life, so the legs simply stand propped against the wall.

Adding to my pain, I learn that Lecia has understandably removed me from her health insurance. I have coverage from a Medicare-Advantage plan, but her coverage has paid for all my co-pays. Now I must also add this expense to my growing list of monthly costs and frustrations.

The state agency seems to know something is not quite right regarding my aide and they send out a nurse to evaluate my situation. They determine I need someone other than Tina to help me. I vehemently push back. Tina is working out quite well, I tell them.

Of course, I do not want to lose Tina. She satisfies too many of my destructive impulses and desires. For this low point in my life, she is perfect.

As if things cannot get any worse, in September 2009 my mother dies. Having no real emotional connection to her, I am more relieved than sad, but her death causes a rather explosive reaction from my father. Since he has never really learned how to handle his emotions, he lashes out at my sister and then at me. I finally realize that this is his way of grieving. Interestingly, this starts a new chapter in our relationship. After a rather tense talk, we agree to have a more open-discussion relationship. We agree that we can say whatever we want to the other and it is simply accepted and processed. No more big fights and conflicts. We just get everything out into the open.

I finally cannot maintain making the payments on my car: between the costs of the additional co-pays, my drinking and my drugs I have no choice but to stop payments on my car.

I sit alone in my apartment wondering how everything went so wrong. Instead of dealing with it, processing it and working my way through it, I just sit back and drink and smoke even more. In every way possible, I am passively-aggressively trying to commit suicide. Each day as I put myself to bed, I pray I will not wake up the next morning. I just want the pain to stop.

CHAPTER 10:
Tribulations & Miracles
APRIL 10, 2010

I lie in my bed with my head on the pillow and pray for peace. I want peace so that I can sleep. At this point, though, peace is somewhat of a delusion considering the abyss I have created for myself. I have scrambled things to the point that I cannot fathom a way out. "Please Lord, help me." I silently pray and gratefully weep.

I do not desire fame or fortune, only peace. I want my bills paid, food on my table and gas in my car.

My life now is primarily one of self-destruction and debauchery. I am convinced, at this point, that peace is only available to me on the other side. Yet I pray anyway.

I regularly call my father. He listens quietly to my problems, my angst, and my pleas, saying little. He lets me talk through my issues, patiently waiting for me to arrive at my own sound conclusions.

In trying to process all that has happened to me, I teeter-totter between insanity and sanity. I think about doing something wild: I want to streak naked through the neighborhood (in my power chair, of course). But then in my sane moments, I end up in prayer. I pray for some sort of salvation from my mired mess of a life.

In my heart, I know that God has already planted the seeds to my ultimate path, but I do not yet want that path badly enough to face and overcome my own demons. I have to earn that path and the peace that comes from it.

It is late in the evening on April 10 when I realize I have not as yet made my daily run to the local service station for my evening beer. It is quite cold and I wrap myself in warm clothing and set off up the street in my power wheelchair, oblivious to what awaits me there.

As I approach the station store, I briefly notice a car parked outside with its doors open. I dismiss the warning and approach the shop doors. As I get quite close, the doors burst open ejecting two giants of men. They are the occupants of the car and had entered the store to steal beer from a display. The clerk of the shop, realizing what is happening, tried to reach the electronic door lock. The men panicked and that is when the doors flew open with the two of them rapidly exiting. But I am in the way. The glass doors first hit my hand holding the control joystick of my chair, they then hit my stumps and finally my head. The force of the impact is so great that the glass in the door cracks. The two men run past me, jump into their car and speed off.

The Manager of the station calls the police and they arrive to take the incident report.

By the time the drama ends, it is well past 10:00pm and therefore, I am unable to buy that beer which had initiated this evening foray.

The Manager is nice enough to give me a cup of coffee and a hot dog for the inconvenience, but it is the beer I crave.

Ten days later on April 20, 2010 I awake hungry. I know that I have a blood test scheduled for this morning, so I decide to first get some quick food back at that same station. As I enter the station lot, it is busy with various morning commuters filling their gas tanks. I enter the store, buy a few food items, and leave.

I rapidly motor across the lot. I am not giving the proper attention to my path and at that moment, my power wheelchair's front wheel hits the curb that separates the parking area from the driveway into the car wash. I am clearly not prepared for the crash, and upon impact, my body is ejected from the chair onto the concrete below. I tumble forward and roll across the concrete as if I am a loose basketball.

Those pumping gas stop and watch with horror as this happens, unsure of what exactly to do.

The Manager of the shop runs out to help me. I assure her that I am not hurt, but nevertheless, she calls 911. In a short time, the paramedics arrive and check me over. I crawl back to my power wheelchair, survey the damage and see that one of the front wheels is completely broken off my wheelchair.

Now what am I going to do?

As I sit here, stunned and frustrated, wondering just how much worse can my life get, the owner suggests we go back inside the store. She walks ahead of me while I quickly crawl behind her. Once in the store, I follow her behind the counter. She produces a blanket and offers it to me. I wrap the blanket around me and pull out my Blackberry. I call the para-transport call service but am told it will take some time before they can pick me up. Not wanting to wait, I begin texting others I know hoping someone will take pity upon me and come take me home.

As I sit, I feel that my life cannot possibly get any worse. I feel completely helpless.

But as I sit there, God creates a miracle, He sends an angel to me, although one I cannot yet fully understand.

After a several minutes pass, a well-dressed gentleman enters the station shop and explains to the clerk that he is having problems pumping gas. As they are talking, I notice him looking at me. They review several of the steps together and the man walks back out to his car.

This scenario replays itself about five times. Each time he enters the store, there is yet another problem. But each time he enters, he sees me sitting there pathetically on the floor with this blanket wrapped around me.

On his last entry into the shop, he walks over to me, leans down and hands me his business card. He says to me, in a very kind and genuine voice, "If there is ever anything I can do for you, my private cell phone number is on the back of the card, please call me." I take the card from him and I notice that his name is Joey Goss. His name means nothing to me, but I place the card in my wallet and quickly forget about it.

I go back to texting and finally reach Tina. She takes sympathy on her best client and comes down to the station. She has a small SUV and suspects we can load my power chair into the back. After attempting several approaches, it becomes obvious that we alone simply cannot do this. Sitting there, I have a sudden epiphany. I wonder if I shift the seat of the chair, will it take the primary weight off the front wheels and put it onto the back wheels? With that shift, maybe I can ride the chair home myself.

I make the adjustment, discover that it works and I proudly ride my chair, on only three wheels, around the station lot ensuring I will be able to make it back to my apartment.

With its success, Tina agrees to walk along beside me back to my apartment. Once in the apartment, Tina returns to the gas station to retrieve her car.

Sitting in my apartment I re-assess my situation. Now I have a broken power wheelchair and, like my chair, I too am totally broken. At this point I know only one thing. "This is not the life I want. This is not me. I want more, not everything, just a peaceful life."

Since my accident, my life questions have always been the same: "Who wants a man with no legs, no job, no home, no car, and no money?" I finally decide in my prayers that I need to ask better questions and seek better answers. Instead of merely looking to God to solve my problems, I decide it is time that I take personal responsibility and instead begin asking for guidance and wisdom.

"Lord, how do I get out of this mess?" I implore.

Bless my dad's heart, he listens patiently as I whine and complain once again. I'm sure he knows that the first step I must take is to stop trying to escape the pain of life and start dealing with it, but he knows it is an answer I must reach on my own.

With my troubles managing money and the persistent drug-induced haze in which I live, my life gets just a little bit darker today when my car is repossessed. My specially outfitted car, with the hand controls that allow me to drive, is taken away.

I sit and can almost see the walls moving in to crush me. My spirit is already destroyed; all that is left is the outer shell of my legless body.

I once again whine to my father and, as usual, he listens patiently and says little. But in telling Tina what has happened, she pushes and convinces me to do whatever is necessary to save my car. In yet another frantic call to my father, he agrees to loan me $900.00. I get into my Power wheelchair and speed down the street to Wal-Mart. With only minutes to spare, I arrive at the Western Union counter and wire the money to the bank. With the payment made, the bank contacts the towing company to release my car.

In what seems to be yet another miracle, a man with the recovery/towing company has a relative with a power chair. He noticed the special controls in my car and since they were not really part of the recovery, he ordered someone in the lot to remove them. When he gets word from the bank that my car is to be released, he is kind enough to contact me, telling me he will bring the car and the controls back to me. If you know anything about recovery companies, you will also see this as a miracle, as recovery companies never "return" your car.

Along with the car, they return the special hand control equipment.

So, I have my car, but I cannot drive it without the hand controls. I am happy and frustrated at the same time.

After sitting and fretting for a couple of days, yet another miracle happens. A driver from the recovery company comes to my apartment and offers to re-install the removed equipment, no doubt at the prompting of the owner.

As grateful as I am for his efforts, the job is not done exactly right. With Tina's continued encouragement, I call the company which originally installed the equipment. They ask me to bring the car to them. "How can I possibly drive my car to the garage without the controls?" I ponder.

Well, my motivation to have my car working again trumps all common sense. I climb into my car with my pair of canes. I drive like an old man going no more than twenty miles an hour with one hand on one of the canes that I use to press on the gas and brake pedals. In this miracle, I arrive safely at the garage. It takes only about one hour for them to properly re-install the equipment. It was the longest ride of my life driving to the garage and probably the shortest and most joyous ride driving home.

Once home, I realize that as bad as my money management skills have been, this car incident has thrown them completely off track and I begin wondering how I will even be able to make my next rent payment.

I am sinking further into despair. With everything seeming hopeless, I begin wondering if even God can save me.

CHAPTER 11:
Crash Landing
August 7, 2010

I eke through April, May, June, and July, paying my rent, car payments and food costs. I am merely lumbering along, not thriving and not really addressing the roots of my problems. I am still not facing my inner pain, so I continue living a life of drugs, sex, and slow suicide.

On Friday, August 6, Tina suggests we go to a party. In my current state, I cannot think of a single reason not to go. So, together we head to this party.

The next thing I know, I am awakened by Lady (my three-legged Doberman) licking my ear. I am in my car, but I am completely confused, unsure of where I am and even more unsure of how I got here. I do remember going to a party the night before, but have no memory of what happened there or how I got home. Something makes me sense that I did not hurt anyone and I finally realize that I am alright.

My car door is open and I see my manual wheelchair sitting just outside of it.

I take a couple of deep breaths and "hear" a calm, low voice coming from within me asking, "Are you done yet?"

Never having had this experience before, I am taken aback and quite rattled. It motivates me to get out of the car, allowing Lady to get to the grass and relieve herself and giving me a chance to look over the car, checking for damage.

My car looks fine. So I wheel myself back into my apartment.

As I enter my apartment upset, angry, and a bit in awe over the voice, I decide deep inside of me, *"ENOUGH."* I gather every container of alcohol and every drug (legal and otherwise) I own and I flush them all down the toilet. I rid myself of all pain meds, opioids, anti-seizure medications, all antidepressants, all muscle relaxers, all of my marijuana, and just to make a complete sweep, I also throw away my cigarettes. These are all the drugs which pick me up in the morning and put me down at night.

As has been my pattern, I call my dad telling him what happened the night before and this morning. Where normally my father only listens, he calmly says to me, "Congratulations. Now, lock your door, get into bed, and sweat it all out."

I do fine for the first few hours, but by the afternoon I begin experiencing severe withdrawal symptoms, some are physical and some emotional. I do my best to lie quietly in bed, but a panic inside of me begins growing. It reaches a point where I begin having chest pains. I finally wonder if I am having a heart attack.

I try to relax, but the anxiety will not go away. It gets so bad that I finally call 911 and ask for the paramedics. I get more than I bargained for when the firefighters, paramedics, and police all arrive at my door. There are far too many bodies in my small apartment. I now basically just want all of the medications I threw out earlier in the day.

The paramedics hook me to a portable EKG unit and assure me that I am not having a heart attack. This should calm me, but it does not. The panic and anxiety continue and I finally tell them that I really need to be in a hospital.

Amazingly, while this is all happening, a friend of Tina comes by and takes Lady home to care for her.

On arriving at the emergency room, they perform all of the standard blood tests on me. I wait for quite some time and finally hear very distinctive footsteps coming down the hall. I hear them slow down at my door and, at that moment, a doctor walks in wearing a decorative pair of cowboy boots and a lab coat. His appearance and demeanor remind me of a slow, deliberate cowboy *sans* the ten-gallon hat.

He sits down next to my bed and begins reviewing the results of my blood tests. He knows that I was a paramedic and goes into greater detail with me than he would with most patients. He makes it clear that unless I abandon with my current destructive behavior, I will likely be dead within the month.

He first congratulates me on my decision to get off of the drugs and alcohol, but then warns me in his distinctive Texas drawl, "The next several weeks, if not the next several months are going to be pure hell. *Boy*, let me tell you, it's goin' to hurt!"

He gives me the option of staying in the hospital for a couple of nights or sending me home. He is aware of my support network, especially Andrew and Glenda Bashor, and he thinks it might be alright for me to simply go home.

The Bashors are kind enough to drive me home, but as we pull into the apartment complex I am hit with a massive wave of anxiety as I realize I am far too fearful to be alone. I also think about the weapons in my home and wonder if I can trust myself alone with them in my current state. I ask the Bashors if I can spend the night in their apartment. They kindly agree and prepare a place for me to sleep.

As I lay my head on the pillow, I realize, for the first time in years, that I want to survive. I realize that I do *not* want to die.

The morning comes and Glenda prepares me a healthy breakfast. I am still in a very emotional state and I feel my TBI struggles and PTSD storms kicking in as well. Everything I see and hear has volume to it, from the paint and paintings on the walls to the fabric of the furniture and my clothing. Andrew asks me if I would like to go to church with them. I decline as I am too stressed and uncomfortable to leave the house.

I am okay in their house alone and I try to simply relax, taking one breath at a time.

After an hour or so, the Bashors return, prepare a beautiful lunch and I share the meal with them.

After lunch, I decide it is time I head to my own apartment and try being alone. The Bashors tell me they will bring me my meals for the next several days as my body goes through detoxification. The Bashors eat a very healthful diet and I am blessed that during this trying period, I am getting such good food and that I have such amazing friends in my life.

I get home and crawl into bed. Other than responding to basic bodily functions and needs, the bed is where I stay. I begin smelling so badly that I can clearly smell myself and am completely repulsed by it. I realize that I smell like the homeless drunks I used to pick up when working as a paramedic. The smell of ammonia permeates my skin as my liver attempts the overwhelming job of detoxifying years of drug use, alcohol, and cigarettes.

On the sixth day of my detoxification, I guess my mind is starting to become clear enough to assess the reality of my situation. I look around my room and wonder how I will be able to keep the few things that I have. My brain doesn't comprehend the reality that without all of the drugs, cigarettes, and alcohol, I'll have more money than before.

Medicated David never worried about such things. These normal concerns of others were ignored by me in my medicated haze. What panics me is the thought that I might end up on the streets. I certainly look and smell like a street person, so it seems as if that is where I now belong.

In my despair, I call my father. The man on the other end of the line is not the version of my father I want. I want a compassionate father who will pat my hand and tell me that everything is going to be alright. Instead, I get the military version of my father; the problem solver. When he does not respond in the manner I want, I play the victim card, "Dad, I'm disabled, I have no legs, I can't afford car insurance, and I'm not sure if I can even afford my rent. Dad, what am I going to do?"

My father gives me the advice I need rather than the pity I want. He very firmly, yet kindly, says to me, "David, if I have to come all the way to Texas to clean up your mess, I will <expletive>-ing kill you."

He is not being mean or abusive; he is just speaking the truth. My father says what I need to hear so that I will start doing what I need to do.

Realizing I cannot continue on my own at home, I again call 911 and ask for the paramedics. They arrive at my apartment, I explain my situation, they load me into their bus, and they take me to the psychiatric wing of a local hospital. I am not even sure where we are going and I don't even think to ask.

I am in a mental state with which I am unfamiliar and I am unable to medicate myself as I have done for so long. I realize that I have no idea what to do with my life. I know that I no longer have any marketable life skills. For the last twelve years, everyone has done everything for me.

Even though I have been living on my own the last two years, those two years were nothing more than an avalanche of self-destructive behavior and debauchery where my end game always seemed to be suicide. Instead of fixing my own problems, I kept waiting for the miracle I wanted. What I want is someone to step in and fix everything for me. But alas, that is not the reality of life or the path God has laid for any of us.

Even though I feel anxious and very afraid, I finally realize that I alone must fix my problems. Only I can make the right decisions for my life.

I am taken to the inpatient facility in the psych wing of the hospital. After waiting for quite some time a group of nurses enters my room. Without my medications, life seems both unreal and intensified. One nurse finally speaks, "Do you really want help?" The implication being, do I really want to get better or am I just trying to temporarily get out of a difficult situation.

It feels like a *Matrix* "Do you want the red pill or the blue pill" moment.

"Yes, I really do want your help." I reply.

With that, they start asking me question for admissions. Once the Admission intake paperwork is finished, they proceed with the next, most humiliating step. I am strip-searched in their hunt for any drugs or weapons. From my time in the hospitals, I thought nothing could shame or embarrass me any longer, yet as I lie here naked, I realize that I am wrong.

For my entire life I have been warm-blooded and preferred cool air. But now, with the status of my body, I am freezing cold. I ask the nurses for blankets. They bring two and I wrap them tightly around me.

I drift off to sleep. In what seems to be no time at all, I am awakened and invited to join a few other people in the breakfast room on my floor.

Later in the day, I am asked to attend group therapy with other patients in the clinic. During that session I participate in a role-play exercise. This exercise seems to magnify just how helpless I am and how dependent on others my life has become. Whether or not this is the purpose of the exercise, I do not know, but it intensifies my desire to once again be independent.

This exercise really sets the tone for the rest of my therapy. I want to be clean and free of my demons. I want to be a man again, not merely a victim of my accident.

Two days later another man is admitted to the clinic. He is a flight attendant and becomes my new roommate. We get along well and one night as we are crawling into bed, he turns to me and asks, "Do you know Jesus Christ? Would you like to say the sinner's prayer with me?"

I have said this prayer many times in my life, but usually as a way to get myself out of a sticky situation, in other words, putting on a good show for myself and others. I realize that I have never before said it in earnest. But now, as I pray this prayer once again, I realize how empty I am; it is as if David and David's ego no longer exist. I am laid bare and open.

Lord Jesus, for too long I've kept you out of my life. I know that I am a sinner and that I cannot save myself. No longer will I close the door when I hear you knocking. By faith I gratefully receive your gift of salvation. I am ready to trust you as my Lord and Savior. Thank you, Lord Jesus, for coming to earth. I believe you are the Son of God who died on the cross for my sins and rose from the dead on the third day. Thank you for bearing my sins and giving me the gift of eternal life. I believe your words are true. Come into my heart, Lord Jesus, and be my Savior. Amen. – Dr. Ray Pritchard

Upon finishing the prayer, yet another miracle occurs. I actually see a physical manifestation of Christ. It is only I who can see Him, but He is now real to me and He is a part of me.

I realize I no longer need drugs in my life. I also realize that the peace I have so desperately sought is now within me; the peace that passes all understanding. I lay my head down on my pillow and I sleep. It is the deep, restful sleep that has so eluded me all of these last years.

The next morning, I review all that has happened. I feel I am strong enough to leave the hospital and return home to start building my new life. So, I ask the staff for an Admission review.

The review does not go as I first hoped. I meet with a doctor and there, also in the room, is a Tarrant County Deputy Sheriff. The doctor explains to me, "Since you are a voluntary patient, you can be released at any time. On the other hand, if we review your case and determine that you are a risk to yourself and to others, you will then be committed for at least 30 days. So, do you want to take this risk of petitioning? Or, do you just want to stay here a while longer until we determine when it is your time to be discharged?"

Hmmm... "I think I will just drop the admission review and stay where I am."

I am given more freedom in the clinic and am now permitted to take my meals in the communal dining and recreation areas.

I am finally approached by the staff regarding my discharge. I meet with a social worker who first strongly encourages me to change my Medicare Advantage healthcare back to Original Medicare.

As I sit and reflect on returning home, I wonder if I even still have a home. Have I been evicted? Have my things been thrown out? What about Lady, where is she?

I learn that I have been in the clinic for 11 days. I express my concerns to the social worker, and she suggests that I transfer to a nursing facility until all of the other details can be resolved.

I leave the psych hospital clinic and am transported to a nursing home. I arrive in the evening and after being admitted, I once again call my father. This time my father has the kindness and compassion I wanted him to have during my last phone call. I tell him that I am now in a nursing home. He queries, "Why are you there?" I explain to him my concerns and the unknowns I am facing and he replies, "Well, you can't do anything until you know."

I feel like a child being given instructions as he continues, "You need to call the apartment complex and find out if you still have a home and if your stuff is still there. Ask if your car is still there as well."

I am unable to find the phone number of the complex on my own and have to ask for help. I call the complex and the girl answering the phone seems quite happy to hear from me. I tell her my concerns and she replies, "Yes, your place is still yours, your things are still in place and your car is in the parking area. You are good to go!"

Since I have everything in order, the nursing facility agrees to discharge me and send me home.

Before actually discharging me, the Administrator of the facility gives me an option, "Mr. Norcott, you can continue living here and you will be given an allowance of $60 per month. We can assign you a case manager who will manage all your affairs. When the time is right, they will help you find a new place to live and continue working with you."

I return to my room to mull over my options. I realize that I am rather annoyed and offended by the suggestion that I need someone to manage my affairs. I decide I need to get back to my own place and learn to manage my own life. I need to be independent again!

With newly found determination, I return to the Administrator's office and I clearly tell him, "You can help me go home, or you can watch me leave, and once I do get home, I will bring back your wheelchair!"

He gives me a long look and replies, "Mr. Norcott, why don't you go to the dining room and get something to eat. Let me make a few phone calls. Come back when you finish your meal and we'll review your options."

One problem in my wheeling out of the facility on my own is that I really have no idea where I am.

Later, back in the Administrator's office he tells me, "I will sign you out, Against Medical Advice, because I have no care plan in place for you. If you will be patient, the maintenance man has agreed to drive you home in the facility van when he finishes his shift."

I return to my room, pack up my very few things and sit down to wait.

Later in the day, the maintenance man finds me and we head out.

As we leave the nursing home, I discover it is simply on the other side of the interstate from my apartment complex. I actually *could* have just left on my own!

After the driver drops me off in front of my apartment, I hesitantly enter, wondering what I will find. It is all the same and yet it feels like an entirely new place. Now with clear eyes and a clear head it is as if I am seeing it for the first time. It is rather an amazing experience.

I thank the maintenance man, return their wheelchair and sit back in my apartment. I sit here alone and take a deep breath. It is then that reality fully hits me: This is my moment of taking ownership of my decisions. This is a huge moment for me. I realize I must start taking many smalls steps to keep moving forward.

Thrilled to be home, I need to tell someone so I again call my father. He tells me, "Good. Now lock the door and stay in. Don't go out and don't meet up with anyone."

I reply, "Yes Dad I will, and I don't yet know how I am going to do this, but I'm going to somehow clean this all up. I'm going to stick my feet in the mud and make it all happen."

I look around my empty apartment and first wonder about Lady, where she is and if she is doing well. I will have to investigate further when I am able to think more clearly.

I don't yet have a plan, but God begins filling my heart with determination and faith.

PART III:

David, The Bright Morning Star

*"The light shines in the darkness
and the darkness has not overcome it."*
- John 1:5

CHAPTER 12:
Rebirth

"If you don't go after what you want, you'll never have it.
If you don't ask, the answer is always no.
If you don't step forward, you're always in the same place."
– Nora Roberts

I watched a video of a young child, one born without vision. The doctor removed the bandages from his eyes after a surgery that would allow him to see. The child sat in his mother's lap as the doctor unwound the dressing. As the last length of the dressing left his eyes, the child looked up and saw his mother's face for the very first time. He clearly knew that it was his mother who held him, but now he could see her. As she continued speaking to him, his face lit up with joy. He knew who she was by his other senses, but now he could also see her.

I am in the same apartment, in the same body, and I have the same life, yet everything is different. It is as if I am seeing and experiencing all that I have known, for the very first time. I begin realizing just how limited my senses had become from all of the medications and alcohol I had been consuming.

I am still following my father's advice by staying inside and keeping my doors locked. I am in contact with no one except Andrew and Glenda Bashor. They are still kind enough to bring me my meals and make sure I am doing well.

As I review the events of the last few weeks, I wonder how I will keep the promise I made to my father and how exactly I am going to "fix" my life. I may not yet know how, but I am stubbornly convinced that I will find a way.

Now that I am able to clearly see my life, I am also truly praying to God for the first time, and instead of merely praying for God to "fix" things, I now pray often for guidance. I finally sense a connection to God I have never experienced in the past. One big difference is that my prayers are now sincere and genuine. Just as I constantly manipulated people around me in the past, I also realize that I was trying to manipulate God; obviously, with limited success. I fully realize that I am nothing without Him.

I realize how my life has always been filled with fear. With God, I can move beyond that emotion. "Fear that I might fail. Fear that I might disappoint myself. When your god is self-reliance, and you let yourself down, there is nowhere else to turn." – Bruce Feiler

Working to tidy up my life, I finally sit down and begin going through my wallet. I come across the business card given to me by Mr. Joey Goss four months ago. I look at it and wonder why this man would have reached out to me that day. I remember him handing me his card and saying, "If there is anything I can do for you, call me."

"Was he serious? Who is this man, after all? Why does he want to help me?"

There are many things I need right now, but what if I call him and he says "No?" What then? I find myself stepping into that circular hamster wheel, finding reason after reason not to call him.

It is then that I recall the quote, "If you don't ask, the answer is always 'No'." I also ask myself, how would a "no" response from him change anything in my current situation. Of course, the answer is, it won't. I'll be in exactly the same place I am now.

So, after wasting much time pondering my situation, I finally pick up the phone and dial the number. Mr. Goss answers the phone, I identify myself and am stunned when he replies, "Where have you been? I've been waiting for your phone call!" I sit back as if I have had the wind knocked out of me. He actually sounds as if he is happy to hear from me.

He continues, "I'm actually in a meeting right now, would you be available to talk later this evening?" He seems earnest and genuine, not as if he is merely brushing me off. I think to myself, "I have a broken power chair and am sober, where else can I be other than at home tonight?"

I call Mr. Goss later in the day and he asks if he can come to my apartment so that we can talk for a while. Although I am anxious to meet him, I am also a bit uncomfortable. No one has been in my apartment for weeks other than Andrew and Glenda. The idea of having a visitor into my place makes me uncomfortable. But I decide that I since I had the grit to make the phone call, how difficult can a visitor really be? I realize that I can follow this through.

Mr. Goss comes into my apartment and I do my best to welcome him. I feign being at ease. I listen, trying to be open to what he has to say. We review my life up to this point and then he asks me what I still want out of life, where I want to go from here.

Our chat is quite friendly and then his tone seems to change. He becomes more serious; he no longer wants to hear my excuses. He engages in firm, encouraging leadership. He asks me to show him some of the things that I have accomplished for myself.

For so long I have been so dependent on drugs and others in my life, I am not sure there is anything I can tell or show him. Finally, I get the idea to talk about the various modifications I made to my apartment to accommodate me as an amputee.

He looks at me, very intently, and says, "What is the one thing you really need in your life right now?"

I tell him that I recently saved my car from being repossessed. He then tasks me to find out how much it will cost to pay off my car. He adds, "I'm not going to pay off your car, but get the information and we will figure something out."

I also tell him that I need to finish a defensive driving course that was ordered from a ticket I received earlier. He says, "You take care of that and then call Kathy Johnston, my administrative assistant. Kathy will help you with the paperwork and ensure this is resolved."

He continues, "If you need anything, do not leave this apartment. Call Kathy and she will make sure you get what you need."

My initial encounter, four months ago, with Mr. Goss cannot be classified as anything other than Divine Intervention. Only God could send this miracle. Even so, I am having a difficult time believing this is all true.

"Why did God send this miracle to me? Am I even worthy?" I ask.

As I have been pondering my life at home and how I am going to survive, I think about my finances. I am currently paying rent on two storage sheds, a garage, and a car port. I realize that the items stored therein are really of no use to me. If I empty the storage sheds and the garage, I can eliminate the costs of the two sheds and the carport and then actually park my car in the garage. I tell this all to Joey. He nods acceptingly and he tells me to work toward the objectives we have set. We don't shake hands, never sign an agreement or contract, but Joey's intent is clear, "You give me your best and I'll give you mine." It is a true gentlemen's agreement.

Roughly a week later, Joey returns to my apartment with two men and they go to work cleaning out my two sheds and garage. Within about two hours, the task is completed and at least two tons of weight is lifted from my shoulders.

I also finish my defensive driving course. I fill out the paperwork and give it to Joey. He takes it into his office, gives it to Kathy, who sends it to the right people.

These tasks may have all seemed simple to most people, but to me, in my new un-medicated world, they all seemed almost insurmountable. With what seems to be little more than a brush of his hand, Joey has again changed my life.

As Joey is leaving my apartment and places his hand on the doorknob, he again asks me if there is anything I need. With no planning or thought, the question I realize I really need to ask suddenly pops out of my mouth. "Can you give me a job?" The question comes out of nowhere, much as the "Are you done yet?" question came to me the morning after the party.

I continue, "I have no earthly idea what I can do, I have not worked a real job in almost twelve years."

Joey pauses, looks at me for a few moments and says, "You know what? Don't worry about this. I know enough people that we will find a position which matches your skill set."

CHAPTER 13:
Adolescence & Adulthood

The next day Joey calls me and asks me to come into his corporate office on September 13, 2010. He provides me with the address and says, "Come in about 10:00am and dress your best."

Dress my best? I'm not sure I even know what that means any more. I've been hiding in my apartment and only going out to get food and alcohol as needed. Because I have no legs and rarely use my prosthetic legs, I no longer own any long pants, only shorts.

So, I go through my closet and find a decent looking, albeit, wrinkled polo shirt. I also find an iron and figure I can press out the wrinkles in the shirt and hopefully that will work.

The morning of the thirteenth, I get up, clean up, eat a light breakfast, dress and sit and wait. As much as I have wanted this day to come, I am also terrified. Every day since first meeting Joey, I have been waiting for the other shoe to drop. This is all just too good, too wonderful. I keep thinking that all this cannot be real. People just don't help others in this fashion, especially people they barely know.

I finally walk out to my car, get in and drive over to Joey's office. I sit in the parking lot wondering what awaits me. I cannot help but think of that moment in the movie *Trading Places* when the butler, Coleman, takes Eddie Murphy to his first day of work at Duke and

Duke Commodities and Murray says, "What do they want from me in there?"

Like Murphy, I cannot help but wonder if I will be heckled and laughed at. "Will they ridicule and humiliate me?" I ponder.

My mind drifts back to my quote, "If you don't ask, the answer is always no.'" I take a deep breath, fill my chest with grit, get out of my car and walk to the door of the office.

My fears are quickly assuaged when I step through those doors. Erika, a lovely, young blonde woman is sitting at the front desk. I introduce myself and she lightens up with the brightest smile I have ever seen, saying, "Yes, we are expecting you!" She immediately puts me at ease.

She contacts Jimmie, the head of human resources who comes out to the lobby to meet me. About the same time, Joey also exits his office and greets me warmly. They both take me into the lunch room and give me a job application to fill out.

I start filling out the application but quickly realize that even this task is too much for me. I panic and negatively think, "There is no way I am ever going to get a job. I cannot even fill out a simple job application. I have been given this one amazing opportunity and I am totally blowing it."

I also realize that I don't even know the job for which I am applying.

I am so frustrated that I set down the pen and sit back in my chair. Jimmie sees that I am almost in tears and softly says to me, "Don't worry about it. It will all work out. We will find something for you."

I think, "*RIGHT*, I'll be sweeping the floors and emptying the trash cans!"

I reluctantly hand over my application to Jimmie, it only being about sixty percent complete. I wait for her to look it over, smile, and say, "Thank you, we'll be in touch." End of interview, end of opportunity.

Instead, she stuns me by saying, "Follow me."

I am in shock as she leads me into what appears to be a sales office, a sea of cubicles, and takes me to a cubicle near her office. She tells me to take a seat and says, "Don't answer the phones, we don't, as yet, have you set up for that. "

She disappears briefly into her office, and sitting there alone I cannot help but wonder what has just happened? "Am I hired? Do I work here now? "These things only happen in movies, not to me. I try to just relax and am thinking that she will likely try to think of some reason to simply send me home.

When she returns, she hands me two files along with a check list. She tells me, "Go through these files and ensure everything is in each file that is on the check list. Then put the pages in the proper order."

I have a job! Me, David Norcott; amputee; alcoholic; loser. I have an actual job!

I momentarily sit dazed when Erika, the lovely girl from the lobby, comes into my cubicle and asks me if there is anything she can get me. I sit and look at her mutely, as I don't even know what to ask for. She then says, "Would you like a cup of coffee?"

"Yes, that would be wonderful!" I hesitantly reply.

My world has just been turned upside down, but this time in a really good way. I've experienced so much bad in my life these last twelve years that I am not sure I know how to handle or even process these good things.

I do my best working through the files I am given, still in shock, when Joey comes to my cubicle and asks, "Did you bring your lunch?" I am barely able to speak. "Lunch? No, no lunch. This morning I didn't know how long I would even be here. I certainly didn't expect to be hired." I think to myself, "I've barely been out of my apartment these last two years. At home, Meals on Wheels brings me lunch. I muse, "Will they deliver it to me here in the office?"

Joey orders lunch, having it delivered here to the office. While we sit eating, he instructs me, "I want you to stop at the grocery store on your way home and pick up items to make sandwiches. Something you can bring into work with you each day."

As the days pass, I learn more about putting the files together. As I learn and accomplish more, I am given more responsibility.

Sitting at my desk, I remember Joey's earlier comment to me about my car. With everything going so well and my finding a new sense of confidence, I decide to text Joey and ask him for clarification. In a very short while, Joey comes into my cubicle and hands me a check for my next car payment.

Who is this man who just suddenly enters my pathetic life and starts turning it all around? If anything, I owe him and yet, here he is handing me a check. At first, I am unable to even take it from him. I stare at his hand and stammer something, before finally accepting the gift and just saying "Thank you."

I am the only man in the office who wears shorts every day to work and I am a little embarrassed. I no longer own any pants and am not sure if they would interfere with my prosthetic legs if I did buy and wear them. With this on my mind, Jimmie enters my cubicle one day and I apologize to her that all I have are shorts and no long pants. She tells me not to worry about it and simply asks me to ensure that my shirts are clean and pressed. She tells me, "You won't be meeting with any clients, as yet, so there is really nothing to worry about."

I have lived almost my entire life, both at home and at work, in environments controlled by firm, absolute rules. Now I am in a relaxed environment where the only hard and fast rule seems to be, "Do your job." I am both thrilled and a little lost.

A week or so goes by and I am told that I now have my own corporate e-mail account. Not too surprisingly, my first e-mail is from Erika, "Welcome to Cheldan Homes! We are all so glad you are here!"

Shortly, thereafter, I get my own phone extension.

Less than thirty days ago, I was lying at death's door, unsure how anything in my life could possibly change, much less improve. Now here I am, an employee of Cheldan Homes belonging to something greater than myself. I have my own phone extension and I have a corporate e-mail account. My prior home e-mail account was something I used for purely self-destructive purposes. Now I have one to help move me forward into my new life.

I am still basking in the glow of these first two events when I am led into the copy room and shown that I now have my own corporate mail box as well.

Overwhelmed is too small of an adjective to describe what I am feeling.

Before all of this, I felt that I was a complete failure, simply yesterday's trash. Everything I achieved after the accident was merely superficial, including my marriage, and therefore they failed. Because of this, because of my not fully participating in any of them, their loss seemed to have an even greater impact on me. I either did not know how to fully be immersed in them or I was simply too afraid.

I tell Joey, "I am still drawing disability and can only work a limited number of hours each week." True to form, Joey assures me that they can work around this limitation as well.

I also bring to Joey's attention that there are neither handicap parking spaces nor ramps in his parking lot. Joey quickly resolves this with a call to one of his sub-contractors.

Since coming to work for Joey, I have been using my prosthetic legs. No longer are they merely decorations in my room, they are part of my working tools. It is wonderful that the parking space and ramp have been installed, but the reality is that I will likely never use the ramp. It is easier for me to step up onto the walkway than trying to navigate up a ramp on my legs.

Jimmie, the HR manager and Kathy, Joey's administrative assistant, work with me to "culture" my work skills, in other words, my ethics of working in an office. They teach me how to meet deadlines and targets within the construction business. They help me bring a sense of order to my life as well.

I am proud, honored, and even a little amused when I am bestowed with the title of "Construction Coordinator Assistant." I can just barely coordinate my own life and now, here I am, coordinating construction projects!

I am an assistant to the director and the job managers who hire the subcontractors who build the actual homes. As time passes, I am given more and more responsibilities.

I am finally invited to attend the weekly (Monday morning) sales meetings. They are held in the same building, but on the second floor. In some ways, this feels like the first real set back on my job. There are eighteen steps that keep me from physically attending these meetings. Instead, I watch the meetings from a monitor in the downstairs office as these meetings are broadcast to the various Cheldan offices around the State of Texas. I am so close, yet still just a little too far away.

At home I begin wondering about my dog, Lady, and what has become of her. When I first called Tina and asked about Lady, Tina told me that Lady had run away. I wonder if this is true or if something bad happened to Lady and Tina simply did not want to tell me the truth.

Well, one night Tina calls me and says that Lady has returned. I tell Tina that I will be right over to pick her up.

When I arrive, I see that my beautiful, sweet Lady looks terrible. She is thin, emaciated, and lethargic. I am heartbroken and blame myself. Maybe if I had not entered rehab, Lady would be alright. I could have given her the care and love she needed.

But I cannot change the past. I bring her home and later learn that Meals on Wheels has a program to help feed and care for the dogs of their clients. Through this program, I am also able to take Lady to a veterinarian nearby. He tells me that Lady is under nourished and badly dehydrated. He begins treating her for these problems and I take her home to care for her.

At times she seems to be doing better, and then, just as quickly she seems to be drifting away from me. One morning, as I am getting ready for work, moving around my apartment in my wheel chair, Lady does not move. She lies on the floor directly in my path. Now what do I do? I'm trying to do all of the right things; I have a job and the responsibilities that come with that job. I'm pulling my life together, yet my dog needs me too. I feel panic rising within my chest and am unsure as to what I can and should do.

I finally face the situation directly and call Jimmie at work. I explain the situation and am stunned when she says, "David, it's okay, you're good. Just go and take care of your dog."

Again, I am surprised. From my years working in hospitals and as an EMT, no one ever simply lets you take a day off work because of a personal problem. This is all new to me.

Now my problem is getting this one-hundred pound dog into my car so that I can take her to the vet's office.

I ponder the issue for a while before coming up with a plan. I call the office of the apartment complex, explain my situation and ask if a maintenance man can help me. They graciously agree and in a short while a man shows up at my door. He tells me to bring my car around and he will bring Lady to me.

I am slowly discovering just how helpful and wonderful people can be when you genuinely need and ask for help. This is in contrast to my past life where my pleas were merely ways to manipulate people and situations for my own destructive ends.

Upon arriving at the vet's office, I know in my heart that this is her final trip. The vet examines her and tells me that she has not made any real progress over the last four weeks, in spite of all the treatment they have given her. The vet looks at me and tells me that I need to make the difficult decision.

This moment is so horrific, especially since I must face it completely un-medicated, un-soothed and all alone. I am completely awake and aware. This is something I have not done in the last 12 years. As my heart breaks, I drop my head, let a tear run down my cheek, and softly tell them to do what is necessary.

The staff is amazingly thoughtful and compassionate. They give Lady a sedative and then allow me time to sit on the floor with her for as long as I need. I stroke her body and talk to her, telling her how much she has meant to me and how sorry I am to have left her care to others. I tell her that it is my fault and that I must now live with that. After telling her that I love her for one last time, I look at the staff and tell them to go ahead. I am there with her until the very end.

I leave the clinic as a zombie. Reaching my car, I see a girl from the clinic come running toward me. In her hand is Lady's collar and tags. She asks me if I want to take them with me. Part of me wants them, yet the other side of me feels that they are hers and should remain with her. After much back and forth, I tell the girl, "They belong to Lady, not me."

I go home and spend most of the day feeling both sadness for the loss of my sweet Lady and guilt that I am the one responsible for her death. I realize that this is what life is like for most people. This is a clear, un-medicated, real experience. I can no longer escape into a bottle, I must now face the challenges and disappointments in life, just like everyone else.

I wake up the next morning and realize and accept that I must set aside what has just happened and move forward, I must live up to the promise I made my father, I must fully assume that mantle of adulthood. I must face my responsibilities and hardships no matter how painful or inconvenient they might be.

In the morning, I move slowly, my heart still very heavy, but I still shower and dress. I get to the office and when I sit down at my desk, Jimmie enters my cubicle. She says, "Don't worry about taking any calls today, I'll do that for you. Why don't you just focus on paperwork?"

I'm again caught off guard by the kindness, genuineness, and thoughtfulness of those around me. This is the part of the real world I love and never truly experienced before.

A couple of weeks later I receive a card in the mail from the vet's office, expressing their condolences for my loss of Lady. I look around my quiet apartment and notice that her food and water bowl still sit in their same places. I have been unable to put them away.

The following Monday I am hit with yet another panic attack when I leave my apartment early for work. Monday mornings are when the weekly sales meetings are held and I need to arrive at 8:00am as opposed to my usual 10:00am. I get out to the garage and discover that the automatic door will not open. The power to the garages has apparently been shut off.

The problem is that the apartment complex office staff does not arrive until 9:00am, and if I call the Cheldan Homes office, no one will be at their desks as they are all upstairs awaiting the start of the meeting.

My mind immediately seizes up with the thought that I will lose my job. Here I am, doing my best to lead a better life yet circumstances seem to keep working against me. I try to calm myself, but again realize that these are the normal challenges that everyone else experiences.

Finally, staff from the apartment complex arrives and the power is restored to the garage doors. I hurry off to work but do not arrive until 10:00am.

As I walk in Joey sees me, comes over and says, "Where were you?" I take a deep breath and tell him what happened at home and that I was unable to reach anyone here in the office. He looks at me briefly and says, "Well, why didn't you just reach up and disengage the door from the power opener?" I keep my mouth shut, for once in my life, and simply stare at him. It finally dawns on him what he said and how it relates to my physical limitations. He looks sheepishly at me and says, "I'm sorry, you cannot reach it; can you?"

In the past, this type of comment would have triggered me into a meltdown. But now, thanks to sobriety, my mind's filter is working more efficiently, and I know better than to lash out at a man who has already done so much for me.

It is the sense of rebirth that the old egomaniacal, manipulative, self-serving David is slowly being reborn into a humble man, one living within the same parameters as other adults.

I now understand that confidence has to be earned, and earned on many levels. It isn't always just about what you do, but often it is also about what you do not do. I am becoming more than mere bluster; I am finally becoming a man.

My life begins to fall into a routine, as it does with most sober adults. I mainly visit my work, my home, the grocery store, the gas station, I go to my regular doctor's appointments and I see my prosthetist, Mark, as I am again regularly wearing my legs.

I am also reading more. As Joey continues to mentor me, he recommends books. One book I delve into is *The Seven Habits of Highly Successful People*. As much as I have matured, my brain is still not working at the same level as most people. So, for the seven steps to fully sink in, I must read and repeatedly re-read this same book. Retention is still my greatest issue. In spite of the therapy I have received in the past, I still struggle with short- to long-term memory transitions, which impacts comprehension and spatial reasoning. I usually know what I want to do or accomplish, but assembling the steps to attain that goal is often an immense challenge.

I try to remind myself that not everyone retains information the first time it is presented. Some people will retain quickly and others more slowly. I realize that I sit somewhere on a normal, human spectrum and I also realize that I can live with that too.

I have now been working at Cheldan Homes for about four months. The holidays are upon us and I discover that the sub-contractors working for our company send holiday gifts to our office. These gifts include tins of cookies, candy, and providing lunch. Having never experienced this before in a job, I am reveling in it all; I am also over-indulging. My diet at home is rather limited and routine. This continuous feast is simply more than I can resist.

All of this food begins plumping me up, which includes my stumps. So, each morning as I prepare for work, it takes greater and greater effort to push my stumps into the sockets of my prosthetic legs. The additional pressure on my left stump causes me, over time, to develop a blood blister.

Not wanting the party to end, nor wanting to give Joey any reason to fire me, I simply endure the pain and discomfort for the time being.

The blister finally gets so bad and my stumps so plump that I can no longer even attempt to put on my left prosthetic leg. I relent and call in sick.

Without the pressure on it, the blister heals rather quickly and I return to work. When I arrive, Joey calls me into his office. I brace myself for a good dressing down, but instead Joey calmly asks, "What happened? Are you alright?" I explain to him what happened and why I did not come into work. In his best fatherly, leadership style he says to me, "I don't care what is wrong with you, you need to drag your ass into work each day." Again, I am maturing. Instead of lashing out at him, I think for a moment and reply, "Joey, I can't wear only one leg and get around. It just doesn't work that way."

At this point in my life, the only time I use my New Power wheelchair is inside at home.

As much as I have grown and learned about life in this last year, I can't help wondering if it is all truly real. I keep thinking that some unforeseen event will throw me back to my previous, dismal life and all of the bad will quickly come flooding back.

In addition to responsibly paying my bills, another adult decision I make is to start saving a good portion of my money. I have one very important debt that needs to be repaid. I reach the point where I have saved enough to repay my father the money he lent me to recover my car. In addition to the original amount, I add on an extra chunk to cover both interest on the loan and as a thank you to my father.

My confidence continues growing as I approach Christmas. Also approaching is my birthday on Saturday, December 18. It is the first birthday I can remember that I will spend completely alone. I wake up that morning and decide to go to breakfast at IHOP. As I sit in my booth in this bland, commercial restaurant, all alone, I reflect back on all that has happened to me this past year. I am humbled, and yet at the same time proud of myself. Without my dog, I feel as if I have no one on whom I can rely but God. Through this I realize that I have begun learning the difference between loneliness and solitude. I discover that in solitude I also find that Peace that so eluded me a year ago.

Through the challenges and growth of this year, I also understand the reality of Faith. Words are quite different from the application of living daily with God.

As the month progresses, I see New Year's Eve looming large. If there ever was just one day that reflected my previous life of debauchery, New Year's Eve is it.

I approach it with some trepidation, but on that night, I go to bed early and I sleep through the revelry happening around me. I go to sleep leaving the old me behind and waking up in the new year in my new life. "With all that has already happened to me, what will this year bring?" I wonder.

CHAPTER 14:

Full Circle

It is now January 2011, a fresh new year in my new life. This year in Texas is greeted with a long period of freezing ice storms.

My friendship with Andrew and Glenda remains as strong as before, but I am slowly becoming less dependent upon them. Along the way I have also met two neighbors in my building. There is Jan, who lives directly above me on the second floor and Joanne who lives on the third floor. Jan is an assistant elementary school principal. She is a beautiful woman and I find myself very attracted to her. We have talked, but we have never gotten to know each other well.

Joanne is a nurse working at the same school as Jan.

I awake one morning to the sound of the fire alarm in my building. As I lie quietly in my bed, I also notice the sound of water dripping. As my ears focus on the various noises, I then hear a sound similar to a waterfall.

I get up, wondering what is happening. I have finally gotten a new power chair, but one only for home use. It is smaller and lighter than my previous chair. I hear my door open and Andrew calling my name. I enter my living room and ask Andrew what is going on. He tells me that the fire sprinkler pipes have frozen and burst on the third floor. Water is running down the floors in the various apartment buildings and will eventually settle in my apartment here on the first floor.

After time passes, the fire department arrives and shuts off the water.

The next morning, Saturday, I am dressed ready for the day and eating breakfast. I am surprised by a knock at my door. I slowly move across my sopping wet carpet to the front door and am pleased to see Jan standing there. She asks, "Would you like to come upstairs, spend the day with me and Joanne and get away from your wet apartment? Maintenance should come today to rip up your carpet, so, you'll just be in the way down here."

Would I? Um…. YEAH!!

I ponder the offer for a moment and realize that to get to her apartment, I must walk up a flight of stairs. So, I ask, "What about the stairs? What are they like?"

She sighs and says, "They are covered with a thick layer of ice."

Wanting badly to join Jan upstairs my mind races through how I might possibly navigate the ice-covered outdoor staircase. I then remember I had earlier bought a pair of shoe grips for walking safely on ice. I find them in my closet and quickly attach them to my shoes.

Both Jan and Andrew accompany me up the stairs, ensuring my safety. I enter Jan's warm and dry apartment, sit down and relax. Joanne also comes down and joins us for most of the day.

As I mentioned before, Jan and I know each other, but not well. She knows I was in an accident years earlier, but knows none of the details. With a lot of time on our hands this day, we talk more about the prior twelve years of my life. As I begin reliving the auto accident of 1998, going into great detail about the time and location, Jan suddenly looks at me with a mix of shock and disbelief. In that moment, she realizes that it was she who lived up the street from where the accident occurred. It was she and her then-husband who were the first ones to the scene after the accident.

Jan lets out a small scream and begins crying and trembling. She gets up out of her chair and walks away from me. I cannot help myself and I too begin crying.

How has fate taken this woman from standing over me the night of the accident to now being my neighbor?

Finally, we both pull ourselves together, sit down and Jan says, "I'd rather not talk about this any further."

In fact, we never speak of the accident again. It is too painful for both of us.

Between the emotions of reliving that night and my strong physical attraction to Jan, I tell her that I really need to get back to my apartment; I am concerned that we are both far too vulnerable. As much as the old part of me would love something to happen between us, the hopefully more adult David realizes that I just need to go home.

My apartment is a complete mess. Both the carpet and the padding have been ripped up. Everything in my apartment is on the opposite side of the room from before and there are fans helping to dry it all out.

The damage to my apartment is minimal, but it creates a certain level of chaos in my brain. I try remaining calm and simply accepting the situation.

While surveying the mess, Jan offers to let me stay at her place. I inwardly smile, but politely refuse.

I make it through Sunday, alone in my apartment, sleep through the night and get up on Monday to face another week on my job.

CHAPTER 15:
Eighteen Steps Up The Mountain

With sobriety comes responsibility. With responsibility comes routine. I now realize that I find a certain level of comfort and security in my routines. So, when there are forced changes, it often takes me time to adapt. I can only assume this is how others live their lives as well. For me, this is all still new. I do find that I am able to channel my addictive behavior from being destructive to instead being productive.

Within just a few days, my apartment is dry and new padding and carpet are laid. As my apartment once again becomes my home, I too feel more normal and at peace. My routine is re-established.

In addition to my usual list of routine stops, such as work, the grocery store, and church, I add a new item to the list. I begin re-attending the Dallas Amputee Support Group in Dallas. Initially, this is quite the challenge because it is outside of my 8 to 10-mile circle of safety. I have to drive to Richardson, a city north of Dallas, for the meetings. I have been to these meetings before but not since I became awake, conscious, and sober. The first few trips are quite stressful and fill me with anxiety. As I continue to attend and make the drive, I am able to travel there without any mental or emotional triggers.

There is another post-medication change in my life as well. For the last several years, I have been sleeping with the aid of a sleep apnea device. It was first prescribed to me after an earlier sleep study was conducted and the results showed my sleep apnea was "severe." At the time of that study, I was having up to 90 events per hour. When first prescribed, it was a miracle device. My previously restless and light sleep transformed to nights of deep, restful slumber. Now after so many changes in my life, my doctor suggests conducting another study.

The results stun both of us! Now that I am off all of my medications, both prescribed and non-prescribed, and off all alcohol, my sleep results are quite different. I go from severe to mild. The doctor suggests I try sleeping without the machine for a while.

It is amazing, after being so dependent upon the machine and now I suddenly do not need it. Even without it, I still have a full night of deep sleep.

The following Monday I again watch the sales meeting in my first-floor cubicle on my monitor, a meeting being held just one floor above me. I decide that it is time to change this. I strut out to the lobby and critically survey the staircase. I think back to early January and ponder, "I climbed an ice-covered staircase outside of my apartment; there is absolutely no reason that I cannot climb this one!" I decide it is time, time to buck up, put on my big-boy pants, and climb the stairs for the next meeting.

I talk to Jimmie and tell her my thoughts. She is thrilled, but she suggests that, for now, we keep this between the two of us.

The next Monday, Jimmie and I walk up this corporate "mountain" together. I fully stun Joey by walking into the meeting room. This is the real reason Jimmie wanted me to tell no one, she wanted to surprise Joey.

I see the expression on Joey's face and it pretty much says it all. He is pleased and proud of me at how far I have come in this last year. I am rather proud of myself as well.

Without the chemical depressants and stimulants, I used to take, I find that I am able to refocus my addictive behaviors. I become committed to living frugally, saving money, and paying off my debts.

I discover that a bag of lentils costs me only $1 and provides me with lunches for an entire week. After a few months I begin splurging and add bacon pieces to the mixture. For dinner, I buy packages of frozen burritos at Wal-Mart in assorted flavors. These then become my daily dinners.

These various routines become my safety net and my comfort zone. So, when anything upsets my now carefully orchestrated life, I become upset. This Sunday is proof. In preparing for work the next morning I get a shirt and the iron from my closet. I plug in the iron and realize that it is not getting hot. My trusty iron has gone to that great laundry room in the sky. Here I am, though, without an iron and with no pressed shirt to wear in the morning.

I know that other non-medicated adults get upset when things don't go their way, but I still feel as if I am somehow unique in this regard. I want to lash out, hit something my fists, or have a hissy fit, but my newly-found maturity pushes me to simply deal with the situation. I first call a neighbor and ask if I might borrow her iron, but after hanging up the phone, I realize that that is really not the solution to my problem. So, I get ready and head to Wal-Mart to buy a new iron.

By the time I arrive at Wal-Mart I have calmed down considerably and feel more in control; though that feeling is short lived. As I find the appropriate aisle within the unending caverns that is Wal-Mart, I again panic as I scan the overwhelming multitude of iron options on the shelves. How do I choose one of them? Which is the best value? Does paying more ensure that I will get a better iron? These questions and many more race through my head, complicating what I thought would be a simple trip to the store. I finally find one of the least expensive irons, read about the various features on the box and decide, "This one will work just fine for me." After all, it has various heating options, it has steam, and it has a spray as well. What more do I really need? I ask myself.

When I return home, my neighbor is there with her iron, offering it to me. I thank her, but show her that I bought a new one and that I prefer breaking it in.

I am still amazed at how kind and thoughtful people can be and that feeling stays with me. I realize that as I have become less of a victim the world has seemed to change. Of course, what has changed is not the world, only my attitude.

The year charges forward and I continue making progress in my life, working and saving money. The summer is quite brutal and hot and I look forward to the cooler autumn weather ahead. As the weather begins cooling, I initially feel more at ease. Well, I feel that way until I get hit with the first bout of my allergies.

I know I need to take some sort of medication to help me through this period, but my brain and my gut together raise red flags warning me not to take any medications whatsoever. The absolute last thing I want to do is form a new chemical dependency.

The decision is made for me when I awake one morning so congested that I can barely breathe; I also have conjunctivitis and an inner-ear infection. I have no choice but to take the day off work and see my doctor. She checks me out and gives me two shots along with a prescription. I tell her of my concerns with medications and she reviews several over-the-counter options with me.

I still worry that being off work will lead to my dismissal. I return home and do my best to rest and eat well so that I might quickly recover and return to work.

The reality at work is that with each new task I am given, I am also given more responsibility. With that increased responsibility I also receive increased trust from Joey. I am now networking and speaking in various groups. Because of this, I ask Joey if I can have some business cards. As before, I agonize over this request for several days. Joey's response? "Sure, no problem." I also ask for a name tag for my uniform and within a couple of days it too arrives.

I finally realize that my worrying about being fired is simply wasted energy.

In keeping with Joey's informal management style, he periodically drops by my cubicle for a chat and a pep talk. He thoroughly surprises me this morning by telling me that many of his customers and vendors have commented to him about the energy and enthusiasm I broadcast over the phone when they speak to me. These small "attaboys" do make me feel good, but they still surprise me. How can a pitiful, legless loser like me really be making a difference in this big company?

I decide it is time to move beyond my standard "look" at work. One day while shopping at Wal-Mart for my groceries, I venture over to the men's clothing section and peruse the pants. It has been so long since I have worn a pair that I'm not even certain of the size I need. After much thought, I select a couple of pairs and purchase them. Wearing pants to work makes me feel more professional and more a part of the company. More importantly, I feel less of a charity case.

One day in the lunch room, Joey walks in while I am standing in front of the oven. The multi-paned glass on the oven door creates a mirror-like effect. I look down at the glass and have my first "mirror therapy" moment. Mirror therapy is used on amputee patients, especially those who suffer from phantom pains. Because of the long pants, I cannot see my prosthetic legs. My mind registers the image as if it is reflecting my own legs, the legs lost 14 years earlier. I actually have the sensation that my legs are still in place. I am all excited and yell out, "Look! I've got legs!" Joey is understandably confused. But runs over and takes several pictures of my legs in the reflection.

It is the fall of 2011; I am at my desk and my cell phone rings. I look down at the displayed number and although I do not recognize it, I do notice the area code is one from my home town in Maryland.

I tentatively answer the phone, "hello?", and am surprised when the voice on the other end hesitates and replies, "I'm sorry, wrong number."

My brain suddenly recognizes the voice from long ago and I realize that it is my son Kyle. I almost shout back into the receiver "Kyle! How are you?"

We both relax a little and talk for quite some time. He finally gets to the purpose of the call. "Dad, I will be graduating from high school in the spring and am wondering if you might be able to attend."

My heart swells. I am thrilled, flabbergasted, and honored by the invitation.

I know that it is important to both of us that I attend, but how exactly will I get there and make this all happen? At this moment, I do not know. But the fact that he called and invited me lights a fire within me to somehow make it happen.

My mind races through all of the things that must occur for me to attend Kyle's graduation. The first thing I know is that I need to talk to Joey. I need to make sure he is alright with my taking the time off work.

Actually, I need to take some time off work to maintain my disability status, anyway. By continuing at my current pace into 2012, I will have too many hours logged. So, taking off two unpaid weeks will work out quite well for me.

Joey agrees and begins coaching me on all the things I need to do to prepare for this trip.

As we come into December of 2011, the holiday cheer and parade of food happens again. This year, I am able to control my impulses to eat everything in sight and I do a better job at maintaining my weight.

I still think the most difficult part of my life, these last two sober years, is fully accepting the kindness of others toward me. Even people I already know. Catered lunches are usually on Fridays. After everyone has eaten, Jimmie regularly boxes up all of the leftovers and gives them to me. These leftovers usually make meals for me for the next several days. In this office I feel loved and supported. This is far more meaningful to me than my paycheck.

As the holidays come and go, I begin making a list of all I need to do to make manifest this fall trip to Maryland. The first step is saving enough money. I know that I cannot afford to fly there, so my only viable option is driving. What would seem ordinary to most people seems almost insurmountable to me. There are so many small, yet challenging, details that need to be considered and overcome. But I work at taking them one step at a time and knowing that I still have several months ahead to make it all happen.

One night while at the amputee support meeting in Richardson, the leader of the groups asks me if I can drive another member to and from his home in Midlothian for our meetings. Not wanting him to miss the meetings, I agree. I am happy to help this man, but the idea of the additional driving time to Midlothian adds additional stress to my life. The two good parts of this task are that by being responsible for his attendance, it assures that I will attend as well. The other good thing is that I am given a small stipend for the additional gas I need for the trip by the support group leader.

So, everything seems to be going quite well in my life. I have enough structure and routine in my life to keep me content. Yet, with everything going so well, I now have time to realize that I am lonely.

In April 2012, I begin looking on an internet dating site with an open mind and meet Shelley. She is a lovely, sweet girl, I like her very much, and we begin dating. I am filled with conflict regarding a relationship with any woman since my past has shown me that I only seem to know how to have destructive relationships with them. I know that I do not want to make those same mistakes with Shelley. Here I am, twice married and divorced and I feel as if I am dating for the very first time.

Our relationship is most comfortable over the internet as we often e-mail, message, and text each other. I am concerned that I am more attracted to the idea of a relationship with Shelley than Shelley herself.

Since December, Joey and I have been having regular sit-down meetings to discuss my plans for my upcoming trip to Maryland. He counsels me in a very fatherly manner, helping me to consider all that needs to be in place for this trip.

My neighbors, Andrew and Glenda Bashor, moved to Nashville, Tennessee a couple of months ago. In plotting a course, I decide that I can likely make their home my destination for the first leg of my trip. I can spend the night with them and press on to Maryland, to my father's house, the next day.

Coming across the finish line at the 2014 Fort Worth Turkey Trot

Demonstrating my new computer knees

My Paddington Bear award along with my hand-pump cycle

Kinsey at our Canine Companions Graduation

Noah and Kinsey at the 2018 ACA Convention in Tucson

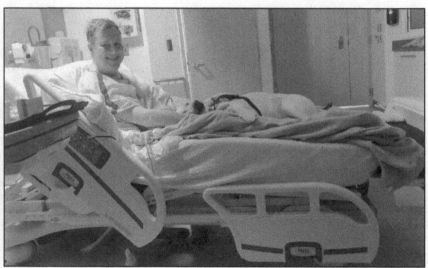

The Author with Kinsey in his hospital bed, post-surgery

PART IV:
Redemption

"This is your destiny,
you're back on your
own road now"
– Mr. Jordan, Heaven Can Wait

CHAPTER 16:
Road Trip & Reunions

"Great is his faithfulness; his mercies begin afresh each morning." -
Lamentations 3:23

The date approaches and I am filled with both excitement and dread. Venturing beyond my "safety zone" makes me concerned and afraid of what might or might not happen along the way.

Two weeks before I am to leave on my trip, Joey takes me aside and says, "David, I don't care where you are on your trip, be it day or night, if you need help, just call me."

This assurance changes everything. I now know that I can successfully make this trip, I feel confident that it will all somehow work out.

Joey, someone I view as a lighthouse in the community, tells me that, no matter what, I am safe. And it is this final fatherly comment to me that seals the deal; he tells me, "You can do this. Don't worry, you will do just fine."

Again, we do not shake hands, there is only an eye-to-eye, man-to-man, verbal agreement.

Beyond reuniting with my father and my son, this is a journey of independence and growth for me. It is my chance to prove to myself that I am an independent man, that I have pulled my life together and freed myself from the bonds of drugs, alcohol, and physical and emotional dependence upon others.

The night before I am to leave on my trip, Shelley comes over and helps me arrange and pack everything. I appreciate her help and enjoy her company. I am anxious to see what might develop between us when I return from my trip.

I pack up and leave my home before sunrise, maximizing the time I have to reach Tennessee and the Bashor's home, south of Nashville. I have a little over 700 miles I need to cover today and I do not want to feel pressured or rushed to make it happen.

Late in the day, I pull into the driveway of the Bashor's house and Andrew and Glenda come out to meet me. The look in their eyes makes it all worthwhile. It is the unspoken appreciation of all that I have accomplished. I can actually see the joy in their hearts. All of the planning, fretting and driving all come together in this one moment.

It is as if I am checking into a Ritz-Carlton, they scurry to get my things and bring them into the house.

We sit down together and review the events of the last two years. Glenda moves between the living area and the kitchen and finally calls us both to the table. Enjoying my meal and the company, I realize how much I miss these two dear friends. I fully realize just how important they have been in my journey.

It is late and I need to again rise early to complete the next leg of my trip. They both work to ensure that I am comfortable and that everything I need is ready for the morning. I take off my prosthetic legs in preparation of taking a shower. Andrew immediately comes over, takes them from me, cleans them and plugs them in to charge overnight. I have yet to even ask for anything, they both simply know what needs to be done and they do it.

They prepare a fold-out couch for me, placing additional padding upon it to ensure my comfort. I am exhausted and need a good night's sleep before leaving early the next morning.

I awake to the morning sounds of a family. Andrew is already in the kitchen preparing a full breakfast for the two of us. I enjoy the meal along with the prayer and fellowship. I want to stay longer, but my schedule is set and I must press on.

I reach my car and discover that Andrew has washed it for me. Andrew also presents me with two to-go mugs of coffee, some snacks, and a bagged lunch for the trip.

God has so richly blessed my life with these friends. The Bashors have provided me with so much more than just physical gifts. Their love, encouragement and pride in my accomplishments will stay with me the rest of my life. How will I ever be able to repay them?

I'm on the road again. My conversations with my father in preparation for this trip reveal his concern for me. He asks me to periodically call him from the road with my progress. On one such call, he asks that I call him when I am about five hours away from his house. He tells me he wants to drive down and meet me half way. I understand his concern, but I have other plans in mind. So, I agree to the plan fully knowing I will not honor it.

When I am about three hours from his house, I call and tell him I am at the five-hour mark and that traffic is terrible. My goal is to completely catch him off guard and surprise him at home.

I am blessed with especially light traffic and I arrive at his house almost four hours ahead of the original schedule. I walk to his door and knock. I hear him calmly yell out, "Yeah, I'm coming!"

He opens the door and sees me standing there on my prosthetic legs. For that moment, time stops and the breath leaves both of our bodies. We stand staring at each other and although my father has never been much of a hugger, we fall into each other's arms and tightly embrace. I can almost hear the music swelling in the distance.

The hug lasts so long that I am unsure as to how much time passes. It might be ten or it might be twenty minutes. He cries and I cry. It is as beautiful as any reunion moment you have ever watched in a movie.

The last time he saw me I was still in a wheelchair. Now he sees that I not only survived the accident, the hospitals, the rehab facilities, and the outpatient care, I have also risen above my addictions. Now here I am, standing before him. In spite of myself, I did not destroy his only son. I have been reborn; I am both my own man and I am his son. The emotion between us does not seem to wane and the hug continues.

The embrace finally ends and we walk into the house. The emotions still cannot be contained and we sit down to talk. In fact, we can't seem to stop talking. It is almost five a.m. before I realize I need to at least lie down and allow my prosthetic legs to charge for a few hours.

I lie down but I am too filled with emotion to sleep. I simply lie here, reflecting on the last 14 years; I reflect on all that has happened and how far God has brought me. I am so proud to show my father how much I have accomplished.

As Moses could only lead his people out of bondage but not all the way to freedom, so it was with my father. He could help lead me out of addiction and self-destruction, but it was up to me to find independence, freedom and redemption.

I am able to spend a glorious, uninterrupted week with my father leading up to Kyle's graduation. He drives me around town, visiting the place we lived and also to the first firehouse where I worked. We get along famously and I have the best time ever. Each morning we get up, cook and eat breakfast together. Some mornings, we also drive up the street to a coffee shop and enjoy coffee and conversation.

One morning, my father gives me an amazing blessing: without being prompted, he tells me how my accident affected him. Fourteen years later, I am hearing *his* side of *my* story. He first tells me that he felt massive guilt, a guilt feeling that he was somehow responsible and that somehow, he could have prevented it.

He tells me of the pain he endured watching me go through the various stages of recovery and, almost worse, the pain of my addictions.

At times he struggles even to speak, yet for over two very emotional hours he continues talking. I am not sure which was more difficult for him, the actual experience or his retelling it to me. It takes everything inside of me to hold myself together, yet I find the emotional walls around me cracking and breaking as I learn just how agonizing these last fourteen years have been for him as well. I have been so focused upon myself that I never realized others were suffering along with me.

For such a usually strong, stoic, unemotional man to suddenly spill all of this onto the table is quite the experience for me as well. It is healing and cathartic for both of us.

He concludes by telling me his worries, concerns, and hopes for me as my life moves forward.

This time is the greatest gift he could ever give me.

At the end of our week together, we attend Kyle's graduation. It is held at an arena and the seating for guests is in the stadium, a structure with lots of stairs. I see the challenge but have no doubt that I will face it and that I will be triumphant.

My father and I are not invited to sit with Kyle's mother, Lee Ann, and her family, which I do not mind. I'm simply thrilled to be here, happy to be with my father, and proud to see my son graduate.

We enter the stadium and I navigate the stairs down to our seats. It all goes smoothly and my heart is full as I watch my son receive his diploma.

We stand to leave and as we begin exiting the stadium, this perfect week suddenly has an uncomfortable turn. As easy as it was for me to descend the stairs, walking up is a very different challenge. It takes energy and focus for me to make it happen. At one point, I lose some of my momentum and I hesitate. I am trying to concentrate and regroup, strategizing my next step when suddenly, surprisingly, my father's body and arms are intruding into my personal space. This then triggers both my TBI and PTSD.

My father is understandably concerned that I am about to fall backward and down the stairs. He is trying to prevent the accident he believes he sees unfolding. I understand this rationally, but my mind is not in control at this moment. I respond by shooting him the worst evil-eye imaginable.

My look cuts him to the bone and he withers. He pulls back from me and I know in this instant I have damaged all of the love and bonding that has happened between us in the last week.

Since we are not invited to the post-graduation party, we head home. Once there, I try explaining to my father why I reacted the way I did. I tell him that I understand his response but I also need him to understand my reaction. Neither of our reactions and responses were rational; they were both impulsive and emotional.

I am not sure whether or not he fully understands, but we are able to make amends. There was such joy between us all week and now it feels as if there is this dark cloud hanging over us.

My time here is ending and I gather my things, pack up my car and prepare to continue my journey.

From my father's house in Maryland, I continue north to visit my sister, Holly, and her new fiancé, PJ, in Pennsylvania.

All during my vacation I have kept in contact with Shelley. As I am driving through the Northeast, I call her. Our talk is relaxed and friendly until somehow, suddenly, my mouth is moving faster than my brain and I say, "I love you," to her.

Upon arriving at Holly's house, I dig the ditch just a little deeper by finding out where Shelley works and sending two dozen roses to her office. We then make it "official" on Facebook, stating that we are now in a relationship.

There is more joy on this trip as I am reunited with my sister. Since she is nine years younger than me, we really didn't spend a lot of time together as children. Our bond has developed more in the last 14 years since my accident.

Holly and PJ live on a small farm. After unloading my car and getting settled, PJ suggests they take me on a tour of the town and surrounding area. We walk out to PJ's enormous 4X4 truck. I walk around to the passenger door and dubiously eye the 44-inches from the ground to the seat. I know that there is no way I can climb into this truck. I express my concerns and without hesitating, PJ walks around the truck, picks me up and sits me in the seat.

Getting out of the truck is no problem as I have gravity working in my favor.

After a long, lovely drive around the area I realize this farming community is causing me to have some Farmer John-type feelings. When we arrive back at their home, I longingly eye their John Deere tractor. Driving a tractor has always been on my bucket list and I hesitantly ask PJ if I might be allowed to drive it around their property.

After a hearty laugh, PJ happily agrees to my request. I walk over, get on and head off across the field.

After driving the tractor, I notice their ATV and also ask if I might drive it. I get a little too bold on that adventure and my sister and PJ have to come to my aid.

The next morning, I am sitting on the front porch enjoying a hot mug of coffee when Holly comes out to join me. In listening to my father talk about my accident and the aftermath, one event seems to be in conflict with what I had believed. I turn to Holly and say, "Holly, I want to talk to you about your having to sign the paperwork to have my leg removed while I was in Parkland Hospital." The expression on her face tells me that I just touched a sore nerve with this question. "Holly, I want to be quite clear, you did what was absolutely necessary; there was no other option. I know it put you in a rather difficult position, but you did the right thing. I hold no grudge or animosity against you. You signed the paperwork based on the recommendation of the doctors and I know you did it because you love me and you wanted to do the right thing."

She becomes emotional and tearful as I say this all to her. I don't think I fully realized until this moment the pain and guilt she has been carrying with her. It is time, though, for her to set that all aside and for both of us to move forward.

The next morning, Holly has yet another surprise for me and she tells me that we will be going to a lake, about two hours away, for a day of boating. Drive a boat? Yes, there is yet another bucket-list item I want to live. Out on the lake I am in absolute heaven as I crash along the swells of the lake motoring in this power sports boat.

Holly, not wanting me to be the only one having fun and checking items of a bucket list, asks for a favor of her own. She says, "Would it be alright if I push you off the boat and into the water?"

Not being able to think of a reason why not, I gleefully agree.

I get ready on the railing of the boat; she approaches me and SPLASH! I'm in the lake.

We return home feeling a good kind of exhaustion, we have dinner and sit down in front of the television. PJ puts on a movie and we blissfully watch in silence.

I'm leaving in the morning so I start saying my goodbyes to Holly before going to bed. Holly is definitely NOT a morning person so I strongly doubt she will be up before I leave.

I am mistaken, though. When I get up in the morning, both Holly and PJ are awake and preparing a hearty breakfast for us all.

My travel objective today is to get to the Nashville area of Tennessee, find a motel, and spend the night. Most people will not see my challenge in this, but since my accident, I have never gotten my own motel room and my mind spins wildly over a variety of "what if" scenarios. What if no rooms are available? What if there are only rooms on the second floor? What if there are no handicapped facilities? What if there is not enough space in the room for me to comfortably navigate? I am also anxious about having no one to help me if necessary. I need to get my bag into the room, clean my prosthetic legs, and plug them in for the night. How am I going to make all of this happen on my own?

I decide I need to just sit back, relax, and drive. I will have to face those challenges when I arrive in Nashville. In my house, I know where everything is and I know how to manage my life. Here, on the road, alone, my perception is that everything is chaotic. Without my safety nets, it is difficult for me to remain calm and confident.

I arrive in Nashville, see a motel along the highway, and pull over to check it out. At the desk I ask if they have a room designed for those who are handicapped. The clerk smiles at me and says, "Of course we do!" I am given the key to a room on the first floor, right next to the handicapped parking space and ramp. I walk into the room and it is enormous, far larger than a typical hotel room. The bathroom is perfectly outfitted for me and almost as large as the sleeping area.

After several trips to and from my car to bring in my baggage and equipment, I see a diner across the street. I walk over and have a simple, yet pleasant dinner.

After dinner, I return to my room, shower, and lie back in bed. As I lie there, a smile breaks across my face. Here I am in a town where I know no one, there is no one nearby for me to call should I need help, and yet, I have accomplished my goal of traveling independently. So much of my worrying was for naught. I need to trust God even more than I have. Trust that everything works according to His plan. I need to worry less and grow more.

In the morning I put on my legs and gather my things. After taking my stuff to my car, I keep re-visiting my room, slowly walking around to ensure I did not miss anything. Leaving behind any equipment associated with my legs would be devastating. After approximately three passes in the room, I finally feel comfortable enough to drop the key off in the office and resume my journey home.

As I drive down the road toward Texas, it seems as if all of the weight and stress of the last couple of years just seems to shed off me.

I arrive back at my apartment late Saturday night. I bring everything from the car into my home and put it where it all belongs. Feeling both exhausted and self-satisfied, I crawl into bed and fall into a deep, relaxing sleep. In the morning I rise and go to church.

Sitting in church, I thank God for this successful and enlightening trip. I thank Him for the long distance he has brought me these last fourteen years. I thank him for the joyous reunion with my father. I thank Him for not giving up on me.

Monday morning, I wake, ready to return to my daily routine, and I drive into work. I learn that none of my e-mails or messages went farther than Joey's staff, none of them to Joey. I discover that Joey was under the impression I would be gone only one week, not two. He questions me about this and asks that, in the future, I keep him informed. The previously child-like David would have come unglued and tried to make excuses and place the blame on others. Instead, the more adult version of me simply looks up at him and says, "Yes sir, I'll be sure to do that." At times, even I marvel at how far I have come!

CHAPTER 17:
"I Can See The Banners Fly"

I can see a new horizon underneath the blazin' sky
I'll be where the eagle's flying higher and higher
......
I can hear the music playin', I can see the banners fly
Feel like you're back again, and hope ridin' high"
— Man in Motion, John Parr

It is now the summer of 2012 and I continue living my life, day by day, still staying within my sheltered circle of activities. I go to work, church, the store, my home and my doctor's appointments as I really cannot handle more than this. I avoid most recreational activities as I am working just to figure it all out. I still don't know how to properly budget my time and my emotional and physical energy. I don't fully understand how outside activities can also fall within my "safe zone."

I am taking on more responsibilities at the office and also spend more time walking in the office.

"Isn't it funny how day by day nothing changes, but when you look back, everything is different..." – C.S. Lewis

I begin realizing that responsible, adult, life is rather mundane. I have learned that adult life is a series of day in and day out routines and that these are all very good things. Joey continues recommending and loaning me books to enrich my life. One day at work he comes into my cubicle and hands me *Seven Days in Utopia*. It is about a golf professional who loses his way and his game as he gets too caught up in the money and the fame that comes with professional golf. In an attempt to escape from his failures, he embarks on a road trip and ends up in Utopia, Texas. There he meets a local old golfer who helps him realign his values. In doing so, he again finds his game.

In my continued quest to clean up the mess of my prior life, I work on improving my credit report by paying off old debts. I maintain my minimalistic lifestyle as I get my life in order and cautiously re-enter the real world.

I carefully budget my money, living as frugally as possible. My daily breakfast is merely a bowl of oatmeal. At lunch I continue with my $1 budget of lentils. I eat dinner at home most nights, but occasionally treat myself to a modest meal in a restaurant.

My life is neither thrilling nor exciting, but it is fulfilling and meaningful. My life is real and satisfying. I am slowly growing and fully becoming a man.

One thing that does change is that Shelley and I grow closer and do more things together. I absolutely do not want to repeat the same mistakes I have made in past relationships, so I am happy to take this all very slowly. The last thing I want is for the two of us to end up in bed together and allow sex to add confusion and conflict into our budding relationship.

The garage to Shelley's house sits at the top of a rather steep grade, one that is most difficult for me to climb with my prosthetic legs. So, she is nice enough to give me a garage door opener. Now when I visit her, I can just drive into the garage and enter her home. When giving it to me, she adds, "Always call before coming over. Please don't just drop in on me."

Since her home is not on my usual routes, it is doubtful I would drop in on her anyway, but I note the request in my mind.

In maintaining such a platonic relationship, it almost feels to me as if we are a couple of kids merely "playing house" together, rather than a serious romance. We often do little more than sit and talk. Other times, Shelley cooks dinner for us and she is always thoughtful enough to package any leftovers for me to take to work the next day for lunch. Our relationship seems very relaxed and safe at this point and I am enjoying our time together for what it is.

I am also becoming part of Shelley's life as she gets together with her other friends and her family. Shelley is "auntie" to the children of one friend and the kids often come over to swim. Several times Shelley and I take the kids to the pool. I cannot help but be reminded to my being at the pool years ago with Lecia's children and wonder if this is the start of something much bigger with Shelley.

At this point, though, I have not been around Shelley without my prosthetic legs. She has not seen me in my more dependent, helpless state when I need my wheelchair. I have not even suggested that I go swimming with the kids. I guess this is part of the reason that it seems as if we are just "playing house" together rather than actually being in some sort of relationship.

Shelley is a sweet and beautiful girl and I very much enjoy being with her. I know I do not want to muck things up by pressuring her into the bedroom.

Well, maybe I'm the only one that is thinking that way, because things begin to subtly change between us. One Sunday I am at her house when she calls me from the kitchen asking me to go into her room and her closet to retrieve an item for her. While giving me the information she adds, "Just ignore the bras hanging in my closet, I just washed them and they are hanging there to dry."

I really thought nothing of it, I was just happy to help her out. Thankful that this legless, single man could do something nice for such a beautiful woman.

As our time together is so comfortable and relaxed, I am not surprised when Shelley asks me one day if I would like to lie down and take a nap with her. It is very pleasant to lie there and cuddle. But I keep myself in check and do nothing more than that. I suspect that Shelley might be encouraging me to move toward sex, but with my brain finally being able to control my emotions and sex drive, I am not, as yet, ready to give up that control. So, I act the role of a gentleman and simply enjoy the non-sexual contact with her.

Shelley seems to finally reach her breaking point as our time lines are not in synchronization. One Sunday, standing in the garage together, saying our goodbyes, she takes my hand and places it on her breast. Inside I am screaming, "YES! YES!" but outwardly all I say is "Wow!" I am both excited and confused and I am very unsure of what to do next.

I realize over the next couple of weeks that something has changed. I call her, but she is always too busy to see me. Finally, she asks if she can come over for a visit. I am thrilled as the only other time she has been to my apartment is when she helped me pack for my trip to Maryland.

When she arrives, she is obviously quite stressed and I can see she is anxious to talk to me. We sit down on the couch and she says, "I don't think that this is going to work out. Do you realize how long we have been dating? "

I pause and wait, not sure if she is looking for an actual date or if this is a rhetorical question. Well, I find out soon enough.

"We have been dating for over 90 days and we have not, as yet, had sex. So, I need to ask you to return my garage door opener."

My gentlemanly moves were apparently wrongly interpreted as a lack of interest. I am sad and I know that I will miss our time together, but I am also pleased with my behavior with her and that I kept myself on track the entire time.

I am very saddened by her news and it turns Sunday into a very black day. I mope around my apartment, not sure of what to do or what to think. Finally, I decide I need to talk to someone about what has just happen. I check the time and decide to call Andrew and Glenda Bashor for their perspective.

Andrew's response is not soft and fuzzy but neither is it harsh. Andrew reminds me of all I have been through and tells me, "You know David, this just wasn't meant to be. Don't worry about it."

With this dark cloud hanging over me, I do not sleep well that night. The next day at work is quite stressful as I carry around the sadness of the day before. I realize that it was a few months of good fun and that it did not get overly complex. I just need to be happy for our time together and just move on.

December 2012 rolls around and again I have a quiet birthday and holiday month. Near Christmas, I go through the various birthday-dinner coupons I have received and choose one to celebrate the two events at once.

When I use a coupon like this, I always order a couple of additional items so that I have a bill to pay. I do not carry cash with me, so my only method of tipping the wait staff is via a credit card. Getting a bill makes this process easier.

I finish my meal and ask my waitress for the bill. She smiles sweetly at me and says, "Your bill has been taken care of." I am a bit taken aback but have the presence of mind to think of her and say,

"Thank you, but have *you* been taken care of as well?" Again, with the beautiful smile she replies, "Yes, *everything* has been taken care of." A Christmas gift and blessing from an anonymous customer.

So, I don't even get to use my birthday coupon, but my heart is full as it is such a blessing, especially since I am spending the holidays alone.

With the New Year approaching, I think of people making resolutions and I ponder my own goals. I realize that I am still just trying to figure out the basics, how to live a good life and be a good man. I am not certain how to insert new goals into my life nor even what those goals might be.

I may not be setting any particular goals for myself for the New Year, but that does not mean that God is not setting them for me. In mid-January, I am sitting at my desk at work when an e-mail pops into my Inbox. It is from Brad, the architect here at Cheldan Homes. It is an invitation to participate in a 5K fundraiser run for the Fort Worth Zoo.

I cannot help but chuckle quietly to myself at the thought of this legless man running a 5K race. To share the joke, I tell Jimmie. She replies, "Yes, I am invited as well, but I'm not doing it!"

Her response is a bit of a relief for me. I figure if Jimmie isn't going to participate, certainly no one could possibly expect me to do so. I do briefly think about the various amputee athletes I have met, known, and read about over the years, but this race is so far out of my "safety zone" that I have absolutely no intention of participating.

Later in the day, I run into Brad in the hallway on my way to the lunchroom. He enthusiastically asks me, "Are you going to do the 5K run?"

At this point in time, I am regularly wearing long pants to work and I briefly wonder if everyone has forgotten my physical limitations.

"Um, Brad. No. Remember, I have no legs."

Brad's response causes my heart to soar. "David, you are part of the office and I want you to be included!"

Something about Brad personally approaching me and asking me to join in with the others has a tremendous impact. I'm left confused and unsure of what to do, but the triggers in my head keep echoing the same words over and over again, "No, no, I'm not doing that!"

Over the next several days, there are other words echoing in my head. God seems to be strongly encouraging me to take part in this event. Part of me is silently cursing Brad for adding this confusion and chaos into my neatly ordered life. But God's voice becomes clear and I finally feel that I can argue no longer.

I submit to God's will and walk to my computer. I log onto the website and register for the run.

In the lunch room I see Brad and proudly announce to him, "Brad, I've signed up for the race!" Brad lights up like the Fourth of July and says, "GREAT!" His spirit, his eyes, his smile, and his face all shine like the sun.

I'm still not quite sure what I have gotten myself into, but I simply cannot fight God's will any longer.

I signed up…. now, what do I do? How do I make this all happen? I'm elated, proud, and confused all at the same time. So, returning to my safety zone, I call Mark to get his input. I need help, but I also need the encouragement I am confident Mark will provide.

I dial Mark's number and when he answers, I excitedly tell him, "Mark, guess what? I've signed up to be in the Fort Worth Zoo's 5K run!" His response is less than encouraging, "Great! Get started." And he hangs up on me. I'm stunned and in total disbelief. I thought Mark would be thrilled and encouraging. Instead, he seems to simply dismiss my news as if I am giving him a weather report.

Something is just not quite right, I decide. This is not Mark, not how he should reply. So, I stubbornly call him back and repeat my news. His response does not change, "Great! Get started." He again hangs up the phone.

I am sitting at my desk feeling sullen and dejected when Joey walks into my cubicle. I tell him what has just happened and Joey says to me, "David, don't worry about it. Don't take this personally."

The next morning Mark calls me and says, "David, I am really sorry. Yesterday, I had a full schedule and also had four walk-ins needing care. I simply did not have the time to talk to you right then. But, David, Congratulations on signing up for the race! I'm very proud of you. Now we need to put together a training schedule and get you going on this!"

Feeling much better about my decision, I begin researching training schedules recommended by Mark. Going regularly to a gym is essential, but I am not a member of a gym and really do not want the monthly expense of belonging to one.

My mind drifts to the fitness center in my apartment complex. Hey! I'm already paying for that and it is free for me to use!

Going to the fitness center presents challenges to me, challenges unique to me and my situation. Where ever I go, whether it be work, the doctor, the market, or any other destination, there are people around, an audience, so to speak. Usually, though, the fitness center sits empty and if I go there, I will be alone.

I need an audience neither for my ego nor my pride. I view an audience as a safety net. In case of an emergency, it is comforting to have people around me. I will be going to the fitness center in the evening, when it is dark. For a moment, I am overwhelmed by this one step and my instinct is to back out of the entire race.

Thankfully, my brain trumps my emotions and I say to myself, "If I don't work out and train, I cannot participate in the race. Now, take this one step at a time and just make it all happen!"

The first step I need to take is becoming comfortable going to and from the fitness center at night. I decide to walk over there at the same time each evening, the time when I plan to work out. I don't even go into the center; I merely sit outside on the bench. This is how fearful I am of this challenge. After sitting a while, I get up and return to my apartment. At this point in time, I am still walking with one cane.

I continue with these nightly visits to the fitness center for one week. By the end of that week I realize, "Hey, I can do this!"

So, after a week of walking back and forth to the fitness center, I actually enter the gym and step up onto the treadmill. I start the treadmill and my plan is to walk my first mile. It takes me about one hour to complete the task, but this is quite the milestone for me.

When finished, I look as if I have done a far greater workout than simply walking one mile. I am drenched in sweat and my stumps, hips, and butt cheeks all hurt. I sit down to dry off and relax. While sitting, my body becomes tight and the soreness is amplified. Now I am hit with yet another small panic attack, "How am I going to walk back to my apartment? Do I even have the strength?"

Not really having a choice in the matter, I stand up, gather my courage, and set off walking.

I survive the walk and, once in my apartment, sit down in my office chair. I have to sit for about 20 minutes before I am able to even get something to drink.

Now that I have overcome this first big challenge, I set a workout schedule of four times a week.

As each day goes by, I find that I am gaining both strength and confidence. I also find that I am standing straighter and I am even smiling more at work.

I continue my workouts, gaining strength, endurance, and confidence. By the beginning of March, I am walking two miles a day on the treadmill. With this new found confidence, I try breaking out of yet another of my safe routines. Up until now, when I go to Wal-Mart to shop, I use the electric scooters provided. The new, athletic David decides it is time to go in and retrieve a few items by grabbing a shopping cart and walking around.

I boldly get out of my car and approach the store. I feel confident and quite proud of myself as I walk through the automatic doors. It is then that I question my decision. The floors in Wal-Mart are polished concrete. In my normal routines, I walk only on carpet and asphalt, so this is something quite new to me. At first, I am not truly walking. I am doing something between skiing and ice skating along the floor.

In each step there is fear and yet there is also tremendous satisfaction. I am pleased that I did not go into a complete panic attack and shut down. I stay in my head and keep everything under control. I just keep moving forward.

I gather the items I need and push the shopping cart through the checkout line. I walk to my car and drive to the gas station, where I get gas and a lottery ticket (why not!). At home, I unload my groceries, get a glass of water and sit down to relax.

What impresses me most is that I accomplish this trip in less time than it usually takes me just to shop and to get my groceries into my car when I used their scooter.

This was quite the windfall for me, quite the accomplishment. What would seem to others to be a routine task, to me is an Olympic gold-medal moment.

As I continue visiting Wal-Mart, I eventually learn how to actually walk on the polished concrete rather than merely "ski."

At church on Sunday, I tell my men's group that I have entered the Fort Worth Zoo 5K race. This launches much discussion and suddenly many of them decide to sign up as well. I am thrilled by their support of my efforts.

My church is not the only place where others are being recruited. Mark invites many of his other patients to join me in the race.

So, even without my efforts, God is building a "Team Norcott" for this race. These two groups, along with the people from work, will be quite the team.

As I look again at the date of the race, April 20, 2013, I realize that it is the three-year anniversary of the day when I first met Joey Goss in the service station. This race is turning into a bigger event than I first imagined.

As much as I appreciate the encouragement and support of those on Team Norcott, it also puts some unwanted pressure on me. I'm still not even sure I can complete the course and now I have a rather large audience looking to me to succeed. I certainly don't want to fall down, break something, and disappoint everyone.

I talk to Mark about my concerns and he suggests I take yet another tack on training. He invites me to come to his office each Monday afternoon about 4pm. He suggests we walk the neighborhood together. This gives me the chance to walk on a variety of surfaces as well as inclines and slopes. So, each Monday, off we go. It is unusually hot this April in Texas so Mark brings along a couple of bottles of water for us.

Mark scopes out the actual race route and tells me that I will need to walk down a hill toward the end of the race. He suggests that I train for that one specific part of the race. He takes me to a similar hill and

I begin my descent. It is the longest, most intense 25-minute walk of my life. When I reach the bottom of the hill, my forearms and shoulders are locked from the strain of using my two canes to walk down this hill.

With two weeks to go before the big race, I re-visit the website for the event and my eyes lock on the words, "Run" and "Race." My emotions take control over my brain and anxiety hits me. I feel that since I can do neither, maybe I should just drop out of the event.

I also then consider that a 5K run is 3.1 miles. My current training is only at 2 miles. I wonder, where is that additional 1.1 miles going to come from?

I'm now questioning everything about the sanity of my signing up for the race. I see Brad at the office and tell him of my concerns. He looks at me, puts his hand on my shoulder, smiles and says, "David, don't worry about it. We are going to be in the back of the crowd with the mothers and their strollers. The runners will be out front. We are just there to have fun, to have a good time! It's safe and it will be in the morning when it is cool."

"But Brad," I tell him, "I've only been training at a two-mile distance. Where is the extra mile going to come from?" Again, Brad smiles and says, "David, just show up. The energy and excitement of the race will pull you along. David, trust me, you've got this!"

I relax, pull myself together and continue my training. The race is only a couple of weeks away and the excitement begins building inside of me.

I show up at the race and the music, the crowd, my friends, Mark, and the excitement all come together to charge me up.

I proudly walk up to the starting line along with my team. It is just as Brad described. We are standing in the back of the pack with various families, strollers, moms, and dogs. Yes, I've got this. I can do this.

The time comes, the tension mounts, the gun fires, and we are OFF!!

I look ahead and see what I had neither anticipated nor trained for - a steep hill. As my eyes follow the hill to the intersection at the top, I see the course makes a left turn and continues up yet another hill.

I have a brief moment of concern as I have not been training to walk up a hill, but the adrenaline is coursing through my body and instead of melting down, I hit the turbo-charger button in my brain and body and I steam-roll my way up that hill.

Since this is my first race, I am not familiar with the concept of "pacing yourself" and I simply continue my charge to the top of the hill. I am moving with such determination I actually move ahead of my team. Mark stays with me but then begins running back and forth from my position to his other clients who are farther back in the crowd.

I'm thirsty and begin drinking water, but I am so high on adrenaline that I just keep moving forward.

I make very good time along the course but my team eventually catches up to me. Since we went up a hill, the obvious final step is that we will all need to come back down a hill. I reluctantly approach the downhill segment of the course. My "team," sensing my apprehension, rallies around me in an attempt to shoulder me down the hill like an injured soldier.

With my prosthetic legs and my canes, I quickly realize that this is not a good strategy and tell everyone, "No, this is not going to work." I love them all for trying to help me, but this is something I simply have to do on my own.

I do not know how much time passes as I struggle down the hill, but it seems to take the better part of one hour. I proudly make it to the base and back to a level surface. I have done so well throughout the race, but now I am extremely fatigued. I take a step forward, trip, and fall down. As everyone turns to me, I loudly declare, "No, don't help me," I get back up and continue the course. But I do not have the energy to pick my foot up high enough and my toe again catches on something and once again my body meets the pavement.

I pick myself up yet again as we approach the final turn to the finish line. We all can see the Start/Finish balloon arch and can see that they are already deflating and collapsing it.

My heart falls within me. I've gone to all this work and effort; I've come this far and I am too late. I won't get to make my triumphal entrance into Jerusalem; I was not fast enough. This, of course, feeds back into my self-doubt that I am not good enough to do anything. I did not say anything to anyone, but I think everyone felt my pain and disappointment at that moment.

A member of my team runs ahead and asks the timer to please blow the arch back up so that we all can walk through it. We were the very last people in the race, and so, they kindly accommodated us.

I see the arch re-inflate and I know that this is my moment. I again hear the music, the applause, and I feel the love and encouragement of everyone around me. My sixteen weeks of training, self-doubt, anticipation, and excitement all come together as I walk beneath that arch with my heart bursting through my chest. I am finishing something I started, something I committed myself to doing, something that I didn't really feel was even possible. I am so thrilled that I am no longer in the same pain I was at the bottom of the hill.

Once passing beneath the arch, someone grabs a chair, setting it nearby for me to use. I am brought water, a banana and a protein bar. I sit there just basking in the afterglow of my success.

As I sit, my stumps and my thighs begin screaming at me. This brings up a familiar problem, "How will I now get back to my car?"

Summoning up as much grit as possible, I grab my two canes and stand up. I don't really walk to my car, I waddle.

Once back at my apartment, I walk through my door, walk into the kitchen, pour myself a large glass of water and sit down. I cannot move nor do I want to move. I finally get up after about five hours!

I realize that I completed the race, all 3.1 miles, in the same amount of time I had been walking the 2 miles on the treadmill. Somehow, that extra mile I feared just happened. It was miraculously inserted into my training time. Brad was right, "I've got this!"

I finally realize I am hungry and that I have not yet had a "Victory Dinner." I go through my stack of coupons and find one for a new restaurant near me. I drive to the restaurant still fatigued and sore. As I walk into the restaurant, I must look as if a strong wind is buffeting me from side to side.

I enjoy my meal, go home, start some laundry, and go to bed.

The next morning, I get up and go to church. One of the men in my group had taken some pictures at the race and he does a short presentation. He makes a point about me being in this race and then being here in church today.

I have never worked so hard and earnestly while being so aware and conscious. The satisfaction of this achievement is so great that I cannot fully process or accept it. It is just too big and too momentous for me to understand. It will take time, as growth is usually a slow process.

CHAPTER 18:
Homecoming

With the race behind me, I return to my usual routine and learn that my sister, Holly, and her fiancé, PJ, are being married in June. She invites me to the wedding and I begin making plans to attend.

Through Kathy at work, I am given an airline employee pass from her brother, Mike Camfield. I am thrilled as I will incur minimal costs going to Pennsylvania and without having to drive.

Initially, I was simply to attend the wedding as a guest, but as the date draws near, some of the wedding party is forced to back out, creating vacancies. Not only am I asked to be a groomsman, so is my son Kyle. On the bride's side, my ex-wife Lee Ann and my daughter Meghan are also invited to be in the wedding party.

With my family's history as well as the current dynamic, I am concerned this trip could turn into a Jerry Springer moment.

At this point in time, my daughter Meghan and I are estranged with a capital "E," because we both choose to be. Meghan was only 14 months old when I moved to Texas, so we never really developed a relationship with each other. This was made even more difficult with my brain injury and then with my marrying Lecia and having her family around me. Over the years, I did make some rather pitiful attempts to change all of this, but they were unsuccessful.

Growing up, I was not there for her. She had no father to love her, take her to father/daughter dances and so forth. She is understandably disappointed in me and I really don't know, at this point, how to reconcile with her. So, we both just keep our distance.

In all fairness, her mother tried encouraging Meghan to have a relationship with me, but the geographical distance between us definitely has not helped. So, the chasm just continued growing.

In June 2013, I fly to Pennsylvania to attend the wedding. Upon arriving at the Dallas Fort Worth (DFW) airport, I learn that my free pass allows me to sit in first class. Wow, what a treat!

As my flight whisks me to the northeast, I continue thinking about this odd mix of relatives in the wedding party and become concerned for Holly and PJ as to whether or not this will work out. That last thing a bride wants at her wedding is family drama.

One night before the wedding, I am out driving with my sister in her truck. It is quite late and I am very tired. She turns into a gas station for gas. I open my door and turn to get out so that I can help her. But, as I ease out of the cab and onto the ground, my fatigue overwhelms me and I fall to my knees.

Not wanting a brother/sister moment to pass me by, I turn around and yell, "Dammit Holly! Why did you push me out of the truck?"

Holly gets this look on her face, a mix of horror and anger. I am sure she would like to kill me at this very moment as she sees everyone in the lot glaring at her, including two Paramedics in their Bus. Remorse sweeps over me and I yell out, "It's alright. No problems. I'm good!"

We get the gas and return to the house. We find everyone sitting outside around a lit fire pit. Continuing my fun, I march up to PJ and say, "I don't know if I am able to support and participate in your wedding."

The look of surprise and concern sweeps his face is evident and he says, "Why? What happened?"

"It's your new wife! We were at the gas station and she was so annoyed that it was taking me so long to get out of the truck that she pushed me! I was caught off guard and fell onto the asphalt. Everyone there was watching and were concerned, but Holly was just mean and ugly about it all."

PJ is briefly confused and then, realizing that I am joking, breaks out in a hearty laugh.

Just then, the light of Grace breaks through the clouds. Probably without even thinking, my daughter looks up at me and says, "Are you alright? Did you get hurt?"

This deeply touches my heart. Even though a part of her is mad at me, there is still a part that is concerned. So maybe, just maybe, this might be the beginning of our reconciliation.

I look skyward and silently mouth, "Thank you God. There is still hope."

The wedding is beautiful, Holly is happy, and that is all that matters.

The next morning I fly home, this time in coach, and Holly and PJ leave on their honeymoon.

CHAPTER 19:
Olympian

At home, I fall back into my usual routine, but now that routine includes physical training and even more foot races. I discover a website that lists upcoming 5K, 10K, and marathon events in my area and I prepare myself to participate.

I am gradually increasing my speed and my distance on the treadmill in the fitness center of my apartment. One day, while working out I realize, "Hey, I want more than this! I want to work out in a real gym! I want to work out and train around others."

With this new confidence under my belt, I begin shopping for a gym, not a gym for handicapped people, like some might think, I want a *real* gym.

Through the spring and summer of 2013, I continue my search, stopping in at various gyms for tours. They are all on my way home from work, along my usual route, yet they all seem the same. What turns me off is that each place is overly focused on money, contracts, and numbers. It seems there is no personal connection with the prospective members.

I recall hearing several advertisements on the Christian radio station I play in my car for the YMCA. I consider this, but realize that it is in the opposite direction of my usual driving route. Even though it is actually the same distance, my brain injury throws up red flags as I am not wont to vary my usual routine.

After much frustration with the other gyms, I finally decide that a visit to the YMCA is in order. I walk in and am immediately made to feel like Norm entering *Cheers*. I meet with a wonderful man, Mike Smith, who gives me a tour of the facility. He seems more interested in me and my training objectives than simply signing me up and getting a check. There is a sense of warmth and community in this gym. Mike offers me three free visitor passes so that I can give the "Y" a test run.

It is an experience completely opposite of every other place I visited, and I feel welcome here.

After my free visits, I see Mike and sign up. This is definitely the place for me. Sometimes the "wrong" direction is actually the right one!

So now I am a member of the YMCA. In spite of all the time I have spent in my apartment's gym, I am still not all that strong. In the 15 years since the accident, most of my life has been either lying around or sitting around. I am no longer the beast I perceived myself to be before the accident.

It hurts my ego that I can only work out with 10-pound weights on the various machines. But I dig in and do my best to build muscle and strength.

I am not at the "Y" very long when I learn that they are the sponsors and beneficiaries of the annual Fort Worth Thanksgiving Day Turkey Trot 5K and 10K runs.

This is perfect for me. I eagerly sign up for the race and tell others about it as well. Some of the men I know who did not join me in the April race enthusiastically sign up for this one.

My training is at a level that I now need to do nothing special or different to participate. I continue my normal workout routine in anticipation of my next race.

Thanksgiving Day 2013 is a bitterly cold day. The temperature is only 28 degrees and I am wearing shorts. The race goes well and is uneventful, except for one unexpected event. I need to use the bathroom but I do not trust using one of the port-a-potties. The only other option is the restrooms in the local mall. I am not alone in my decision to use them and I find a line. There are a lot of people waiting but only one restroom for men and one for women.

It becomes my turn to use the restroom and a lovely, young blonde woman approaches me and asks, "Can I use your bathroom with you? You can use the urinal while I use the stall." I was a bit taken aback, but thought, "Well, when you've gotta go, you've gotta go!" and I agree to her request.

At the end of the race, I am neither as tired nor as sore as in April, but I am very, very cold. I walk back to my car anxious to crank up the heater and warm up.

I am so cold that even the distance from the race to my home in a warm car does not thaw me out. At home, I turn up the heat in my apartment and just sit in a chair trying to recover.

In the afternoon I get ready and meet up with some of my friends from church for Thanksgiving Dinner. At the end of dinner, I am still so cold that I keep my hands wrapped around the hot ceramic coffee mug in front of me.

It actually takes me until the next morning to feel warm again.

One December day, while working out on the treadmill at the YMCA, this beautiful girl, wearing a hat, walks by and turns to look at me. A broad smile sweeps her face and she says, "Hi!" I am a bit surprised but politely return her greeting. She stops, turns around and comes back to me. I think, "Oh no, what now?" She sweetly looks at me and says, "How are you doing?" I awkwardly tell her that I am doing well and she says, "Do you remember me? I'm Renee. We shared a bathroom together at the Turkey Trot!"

I blush beet red and she says, "Is this embarrassing for you?" I laugh softly and say, "No, but it is rather awkward."

CHAPTER 20:

Kyle, Part 1

January 2014 takes an unlikely turn. I continue my life training, working, and growing when suddenly I get an urgent call from Lee Ann, my first wife. She tells me that my son, Kyle, wants to go to culinary school. Then the other shoe drops, "He wants to come and live with you, but he is not sure how you might feel about this."

I am a bit stunned, especially considering all of the past issues between Lee Ann and me about our kids. Now suddenly she seems anxious to get him out of her house and into mine. Although this raises a red flag in my head, I calmly reply, "Tell him to call me."

Kyle does call and we talk about him moving to Texas and going to school here. During the conversation, I ask Kyle to e-mail me, telling me what all he wants out of this.

Late last year, my dear friend and office colleague, Jimmie, left Cheldan Homes. She was replaced in the HR department by Kelly, another wonderful, kind, and thoughtful woman. So, I go to Kelly, tell her of the phone call and ask for some time off.

Several days pass and I have not received the e-mail from Kyle. I am upset and frustrated. I want to help my son, I want to form a bond with him, but can't he even send me a friggin' e-mail? One afternoon as I am sulking about this, I clearly hear a voice inside of me saying, "I didn't ask you for an e-mail, did I?"

Having already learned the folly of arguing with The Almighty, I decide to relax and just let happen what is going to happen. It is obviously out of my hands at this point. I decide to take this situation one day at a time.

I tell Joey of these new happenings in my life and he is quite excited for me. Joey points out that this gives me yet another goal, one more thing from my past that I can hopefully repair, it is a chance to form a stronger bond with my son.

The day Kyle arrives, I pick him up at the airport and we first drive to the Cheldan Homes office. I want everyone at work to meet him. From there, we drive to see Tony at the fire station for a brief reunion. Since Tony is Kyle's godfather and uncle (since I consider Tony to be my brother) and since Tony has not seen Kyle in about 16 years, I think it is a good idea for them to re-introduce themselves to each other.

Once we get home, I tell Kyle that he needs to get busy and find a school. I tell him to jump onto the internet and search for culinary schools in the DFW area. I, of course, hope he finds something in Fort Worth, close to my home.

From the other room I hear, "Dad, Look! There is a Le Cordon Bleu school in Dallas! That's where I want to go!" I hear from the other room. My heart sinks as we live in far west Fort Worth and Le Cordon Bleu is in Dallas. Not only is it not close, but it is not easy to get from point A to point B. But, if this is what Kyle wants, I decide I need to give Kyle the facts and then step back and allow him to make his own decision.

I go over the details of what it will mean for him to attend this school. He will have to get out of bed quite early and eat breakfast. He will then need to catch the bus, catch a train, followed by the rail system and then yet another bus to get to school every day. It will take about two hours each way and that is assuming he makes the express bus connection. I present him with this information and step back.

He tells me that he still wants to attend Le Cordon Bleu, so we head off the next day to the campus to enroll him in class. On the way home we stop to get him a bus and a rail pass. He is to start school the very next day.

I decide a celebratory dinner is in order and we go out for a meal together. Over dinner I sense that something is wrong, but I cannot fully determine what it is. My gut suspects that Kyle has gotten what he has asked for, but that it is not really what he wants. He has finally caught the tiger by the tail and now the tiger is glaring back at him and saying, "So, what are you going to do now?" Less than 24 hours from starting school and it seems that Kyle is having doubts.

I know fully well that I cannot fix a problem or change someone's life unless that person is ready. So, in spite of my reservations, I help Kyle press forward.

Kyle makes it through the maze of public transportation and begins his classes. Kyle comes home after his first day at school and everything is awkward and tense. He tells me that he has to buy uniform shoes for school. I try helping him, but it is something he wants to do by himself.

We both rise early each day; Kyle gets ready and I take him to the bus station. From there he must take the bus to the train station. The train takes him to Dallas and from there he takes yet another train and another bus to the school. After dropping him off at the bus station, I return home for Bible study time and breakfast. After work, I return to the bus station to pick him up.

With an approaching 5K race, I ask Kyle if he would like to join me in walking the course. He agrees and we both sign up for the race.

While walking the course, I am surprised to see that one of the volunteers for the race is Shelley. I am walking along with my son and, at this moment, feeling quite proud of both of us.

I am also proud because I am making excellent time. I admit that the wind is helping me along, but I am about to complete the 3.1-mile course in only 1 hour and 14 minutes. A new record for me!

About one week later, after bringing Kyle home from the bus stop, I decide to head to the gym.

When I return home, I am confronted by a too familiar, sweet, sickening smell. It is a smell that triggers every button and emotion in my body. It is the smell of marijuana and my reaction is both physical and emotional. There is a haze of the smoke wafting across the living area of my apartment.

My heart starts racing and I begin sweating. I walk through my apartment and out onto the patio to catch my breath. I am trying to remain calm, trying to rein in my desire to kill my son, but with limited success.

I return inside and open every window and door. I have to get that smell out of my house. I have been awake, conscious, and sober for four years now and *NO ONE*, not even my son, will pull me back into that abyss.

I return to the patio, trying to gather my thoughts and my emotions when Kyle walks out. I ask him the most obvious question possible, "Did you smoke marijuana in my house?"

Kyle looks at me and smugly replies, "Yeah, so what are you going to do about it?"

My mind is racing through all that has happened to me these last 16 years. At this moment, I do not see my son in front of me, I see only white hot. The only thing I am focusing on right now is his throat. I think, "You arrogant little punk!" and the words of Bill Cosby echo through my head, "I'll kill you and make another one just like you."

I am so enraged that God blesses me by basically paralyzing me. I suddenly cannot speak nor even move from my chair. All I want to do is leap forward, rip out his throat and beat him to a pulp. Instead, I sit here frozen.

When God finally does allow me to speak, he also provides me with the right words, "Kyle, you've got some very serious decisions to make and you are going to need to make them soon."

It is an unusually warm February and I leave the apartment open with the air conditioning off. It is quite uncomfortable, but I am not about to make things comfortable for Kyle right now. So, we both sleep restlessly in an overly warm house.

The next morning, we rise and return to our usual routines.

The next morning Lee Ann happens to call and I tell her, "Your drug addicted son just smoked up my house with marijuana." Lee Ann gets all dramatic and starts in with the typical victim speech, "Oh, poor Kyle." I decide that I do not want to listen to a pity-party song and I quickly wrap up the phone call.

Driving to work I am upset and confused. I know that this situation is bigger than me and is more than I can effectively handle.

When I arrive at work, I go straight into Kelly's office and say, "I need help."

I tell Kelly what has happened and she provides me with the most compassionate, loving response. She tells me that Cheldan Homes has a program through an organization called Marketplace Chaplains. She calls them and we set a time to meet.

I had hoped that Kyle's coming to live with me would mend our relationship. Instead, it has introduced new problems and conflicts. I had also hoped that it might have laid a foundation in mending my relationship with my daughter, Meghan.

Instead, it all seems to have all blown up in my face.

Kyle and I remain in the position of two bulls locking horns. I try my best to help him, but from having been an addict myself, I know that the ultimate decision rests on his shoulders alone. It is not a comfortable or particularly rewarding experience, but, unlike some parents, I know too well the outcome of not dealing with these problems swiftly and thoroughly. This time, though, it is personal!

I call Lee Ann to talk about this and she acts unconvincingly surprised. I am quite certain Kyle's moving to Texas was orchestrated for me to deal with his behavior rather than it being the responsibility of his mother and grandparents. In other words, I was set up.

Berl is the Chaplain who is assigned to my case through work. When he comes to the office that afternoon, we meet privately in the conference room. Everyone at work steps up to take up my usual responsibilities while I hash this all out with Berl. Again, I am overwhelmed at the kind and thoughtful responses from those around me.

Berl listens patiently to my story and gives me encouragement and advice. We set up a schedule to meet every two weeks.

Kyle can fix this problem, but not as long as he continues using drugs.

In May 2014, Mark Ashford calls me while I'm working out at the YMCA Benbrook and invites me to visit with Cameron Clapp and him for a Walking Skills workshop. One other thing that I decide is that it is time to set aside my canes. In my continuing efforts to be more independent, I want to use only my canes during races. My day-to-day life is just me and my prosthetic legs. Yes, I can walk without my canes, with the help, expertise and instructions of Cameron Clapp, a Triple Amputee and Elite Prosthetic user. He is a K-4 (K 1 through

4 Levels of use for Ambulation scale) ambulator and walker, a benchmark to which I aspire despite the fact that he is some 20 years younger than I. He is a great inspiration.

CHAPTER 21:
Meghan

It is spring of 2014 and Meghan's high school graduation is quickly approaching. Since I attended Kyle's graduation, I feel strongly that I should attend Meghan's. In spite of the drama at home with Kyle, I begin making plans for Kyle and me to fly to Maryland.

Kyle suggests that we stay with his grandparents, my ex-in-laws. I am not thrilled with this idea, but considering the cost of the airline tickets, see no other viable path. I agree to stay with them, but I also make reservations at a local motel as a Plan B.

When we arrive at their home, I am pleasantly surprised at how nice they are to me. They really go above and beyond making sure that I have everything I need.

My focus of this trip, though, is Meghan. I want desperately to have some sort of relationship with her. I still think back to that night one year ago when she showed her concern for me and relive just how good that made me feel. I am hopeful something similar can happen this week.

After the graduation ceremony, Meghan's grandparents host a party for her at their house. When we are all together, I give Meghan her present from me. I did for her what I did for Kyle. I gave her a card with a substantial amount of money in it. I view this money as "seed money" to help her begin her future as an adult.

She opens the card and a bright smile breaks across her face. She runs across the room to me and we connect in a tight, loving embrace. This is the moment for which I have waited so long. I am elated and joyous in having this loving connection with my daughter.

As the party comes to an end, I head out to visit another friend. As I walk to the SUV I have rented, Kyle joins me, ensuring my safety. In spite of the problems Kyle and I are having, I am touched by his acts of concern for me when we are in public.

I meet up with my friends and we have dinner together. I have a rather difficult time focusing on the dinner conversation as my mind keeps drifting back to that beautiful hug from my daughter. I silently pray that the chasm between us is somehow healed and that we can now move forward together as father and daughter.

CHAPTER 22:
Kyle, Part 2

Returning home to Texas, we settle back in to our prior routine. Kyle continues attending school at Le Cordon Bleu, but the early and late long commutes begin taking their toll on him.

Kyle has a day off of school on a day that I work. He is still sleeping on the couch as I get ready for work. While putting on my shoes, I noticed a pack of cigarettes on the floor. Something strikes me as odd and I reach down to pick them up.

I look inside the pack and find not tobacco cigarettes, but marijuana cigarettes, the sedative Xanax and a few other pills. Inside I explode as I realize how far things have escalated. This situation is getting worse and I am not prepared.

To ensure that no one calls me a liar, I photograph the pack and its contents. I then send the pictures to Kyle's mother, grandmother, sister, Berl, and anyone else who cares about Kyle and whom Kyle cares about. These are all people, I am certain, Kyle would prefer not knowing what he is into.

As I am taking Kyle to the bus stop the next morning, Kyle calls his mother on my phone.

He has the phone on speaker and I thoughtlessly say to Lee Ann, "You know, your son is a drug addict."

Kyle has a huge panic attack and begins screaming at me, "Pull this car over right now! I'm getting out!"

I calmly say, "Kyle, I apologize. I should have had this conversation with your mother in private." Inside I am wondering, "What do I do now?"

I drive Kyle back to my apartment and contact some of the men at my church who I know have gone through similar issues with themselves or their children. The church men and Berl pick up Kyle and head to lunch. Kyle loudly protests, "I don't have a problem. I don't want to go to lunch with any of you!"

While Kyle is at lunch, I head to the YMCA for my daily workout. I have decided to expand my training at the gym from simply the treadmill and weight machines and I now start swimming. I begin working with a trainer who is teaching me how to properly swim in the pool as an amputee. In putting my training all together, I have decided that I would like to compete in a triathlon.

One Sunday, Kyle asks me if I will take him to the bus stop so that he can visit a friend in Dallas. I figure it is a good idea for both of us to have some breathing room and gladly agree.

When I return to pick him up, he gets into the car reeking of raw marijuana. I also noticed a bit of a belly that was not there before. I assume that it is his "stash" and that he is now likely dealing pot in addition to smoking it.

On Monday we head our separate ways, I going to work and him to school. Again, when I arrive home that evening, there is the stench of pot in the air.

I scream at him, "So, you still want to bring this <expletive> into my house?"

Kyle pathetically tries denying that he has done anything wrong, but I quickly intervene and say, "Don't. Just Don't. Let's not do this dance."

I storm over to the trash can and find the large, empty package that was likely under his shirt the day before. My mind races through all of the possible problems this can create for me. My lease clearly states that drug use is not permitted in any of the buildings and if found breaking this rule, I can be evicted. If evicted, where the hell am I going to go?

Kyle looks at me and says, "You need to watch your tongue with me!"

I glare back at him with a fiery intensity and say, "You know, I think you really need to evaluate what you just said and what you are thinking right now." I feel the old ego-driven, self-serving David rising up inside of me. "Kyle, being a firefighter didn't kill me, being a paramedic didn't kill me, a car accident didn't kill me; even drugs didn't kill me. Kyle, I really don't think you want to go down this road with me. I don't think you really want to do this dance. Now, you need to take the trash out of this apartment and take it all the way out to the dumpster and if you don't, then; 'Game ON!'"

Kyle wisely decides that it is in his best interest to take out the trash that night.

After this confrontation, Kyle stops going with me to the YMCA for our workouts and he also stops attending church.

After the fourth time Kyle has brought drugs into my home, I decide I need to make some rather drastic changes. These are changes to both protect me and to make it clear to Kyle that his actions lead to consequences. I first have all of the locks changed on my doors and then I remove the television and the internet wireless connection.

I bring Kyle home one afternoon from the bus stop. He walks ahead of me to the door, inserts his key and discovers that it does not work. Startled, he looks back at me and says, "What's going on?"

"Kyle, I've made some changes around here. The locks have been replaced so that you cannot simply come and go as you please. I have also removed the television and the internet connections. When you are home, you need to be working or studying.

Kyle begins a long session of pouting that extends into the next morning. When it is time for him to get up and get ready, he just continues lying on the couch. I tell him that he needs to get up, but he just rolls over. For a moment I consider getting a pitcher of ice water and dumping it on his head, but think better of the idea.

He finally rolls out of bed and gets dressed. He is running late and is trying to fix himself a sandwich in the kitchen. I say, "Kyle, if you do not get ready quickly, I will not take you to the bus stop. You will also not be able to spend the day in this apartment. So, you need to get going or prepare to spend the day somewhere other than here."

It is 4:50am and we are in a full-scale screaming match. I will not back down, though. I finally gather my things together; we both step out of the apartment and I lock the door. I leave Kyle on the front stoop and head to my car.

After driving about one mile, it hits me that Kyle is likely to spend the day in my garage. That is also not acceptable. So, I turn around and head back. Sure enough, that is where I find him. I evict him from the garage and wish him good luck.

Where he goes that day, I do not know. I suspect that he walks to the bus stop and heads over to Dallas to school.

Things are tense at home, but he appears to be hanging on in school and I do my best to continue my life as before.

One Friday, Kyle asks me if he can hang out with some friends after school. Again, I think it is best if we are away from each other so I agree.

I don't see or hear from him Friday night or all day Saturday. On Sunday I go to church and there he is. He asks me for the keys to my car because he wants to put his stuff (back pack and other things) away. Because of his rather sluggish behavior, I can again tell that something is not quite right. He is not himself.

My Sunday routine is to go to church and then go to the YMCA for my work out. Before leaving the church parking lot, Kyle asks me if we can go to *Sonic* to get a hamburger.

We drive off together for a visit to *Sonic* and afterward head to the YMCA. I am using one of the weight machines when Kyle walks past me. Yet again, he reeks of marijuana. I am livid as this is a protected and safe environment for children and families and here he is bringing this junk into my gym, my safe haven.

I decide that I am quite done. I call Berl, my father, and several of the men from church. I decide that Kyle will not be returning home with me this Sunday and I let these men know of my decision.

I dawdle at the "Y," letting time slowly pass. I want them to close before we leave. This means we are here for over four hours. When they finally close, Kyle and I walk out to my car. Instead of heading to the doors, I walk to the trunk, unlock it and open it. We stand there looking at each other and I say, "Son, you need to take your stuff out of my car and go back to where you came from, because you are *not* coming home with me."

Kyle glares at me and says, "No Way!" He then grabs his phone and calls his mother. As he tells her what I am doing I say, "Kyle, this is the last time I am going to ask you to take your stuff out of the trunk of my car!"

As I reach for his stuff, he grabs my arm and yells, "NO! I will <expletive>-ing kick your ass!"

I look at him incredulously and say "Really? What did you just say to me? Would you care to repeat that?"

I am actually hoping that some sense will come to him and he will change what he said. Instead, he repeats himself word for word.

I look at him and say, "You need to stay right here." I walk around to the front of the car to remove myself from the situation and I call the police. I tell them that I am being threatened by a person in the parking lot at the YMCA.

In a very short time, three officers pull up. They approach me and I tell them that Kyle has been smoking pot all day and that I am not taking him home. "He can go back to his friends or he can spend the night in this parking lot, but he is not coming home with me."

The police, understandably, are not happy with me. I am putting them in the position of being the bad guys. I am placing the onus of enforcing my decision on them. I, on the other hand, do not see that I have any other options.

They ask me if I want to file a complaint and I agree. After it is signed, they pat him down but find no drugs on him. They are unable to make an arrest, but it provides the opportunity for me to get into my car and drive away.

As I drive away from the YMCA, I turn off my phone. I know I am about to be assaulted by a series of phone calls and I do not want to deal with it right now. On my way home I stop at Dunkin' Donuts and get a donut and coffee. I sit down in the shop and have an imaginary conversation with my father. I realize that I am having to do something similar to what my father did when I entered rehab four years prior.

For a brief moment, this emotionally destroys me. I continue sitting in the shop with my coffee, pulling myself together for the storm that will hit when I reach home and turn on my phone.

When I do get home, I turn on my phone and there is a back log of voice mails and text messages, mostly from Kyle's mother. She repeatedly asks me, "Why are you doing this to your son?" Well, I think, because this is the fifth time he has brought drugs into my world and there is not going to be a sixth. I then call Berl, my father, and the men from church telling them what has happened.

The next morning at work, I tell Kelly that I had to kick Kyle out of the house.

Very kindly, Kelly asks me, "Do you want me to call Berl and have him come in?"

"Yes, yes I do. That would be very helpful."

At this point, I do not know where Kyle is or how he will survive. What I do know is that I can no longer support his addictions and self-destruction. Like his father, Kyle needs to bottom out before he can start rebuilding his own life.

In one call from Lee Ann, she says to me, "You have to help him. What is he going to do? Where is he going to go?"

"Lee Ann, it isn't my problem. He has been stealing from you, stealing from me, and stealing from his grandmother. I cannot allow this to continue. Not only is he buying and using drugs, he is bringing them into my world and that is completely unacceptable. He has even pawned his cooking equipment to buy drugs. No, I will not help him. He is a drug addict and this will not change until he is forced to confront his problems and take responsibility for his own decisions and actions."

Lee Ann tries another tack with me, trying to appeal to my relationship with God. She says, "David, I keep praying for answers for Kyle and I keep getting the same response. I'm told that it is you who is the answer." I sigh softly and think, "Yes, Lee Ann, I am the answer and the answer is to let him fall and bottom out. That is not the answer you want to hear, but it is the answer for which you pray."

Not wanting to listen to me and my own experience, Lee Ann sends Kyle money and I learn later that he is staying in a hotel in Addison.

In a conversation with one of my mentors, I learn that Kyle's personal items must be removed from my apartment. Otherwise, should he break in, he can legally claim that he lives with me and then I would be powerless to force him out.

I gather his things together and then go out and buy him two loaves of bread, two jars of peanut butter and one jar of jam. I call Tony and the two of us go together to Kyle's hotel to make the delivery.

When we arrive, Tony takes Kyle aside as says to him, "you can fix this, but you are the only one. Your choices put you here, but you *can* fix this."

Thankfully, Kyle's mother and grandmother are also getting tired of rescuing Kyle and they too are reaching their breaking points.

If there is a bright side to any of this, it is that my daughter, Meghan, is regularly talking to me. She, too, is desperately trying to get me to help Kyle. Of course, from my perspective, I am helping Kyle. I am letting him fall, I am forcing him to face the consequences of his bad decisions. It is not easy, but it is what is best for him. It is the only way things can get better.

I have two very long conversations with Meghan. I would estimate that they are at least two hours each. I am not going to change my position regarding Kyle, but these conversations with Meghan feel like answered prayer to me.

Like her mother, Meghan's pleas for help for Kyle always include the line, "But, Dad, you have to understand..." Yes, to everyone, I, more than any of you *DO* understand. I *KNOW* what addiction is like.

I know the lies, the manipulation, the deception and the desperation. I do know and I also know that the only answer to all of this is within Kyle. Kyle will only see the answers to his problems when he is forced to do so.

I am also getting annoyed by all this drama, it interferes with my focus and training for the 2014 Thanksgiving Turkey Trot 10K.

CHAPTER 23:
"I Can See A New Horizon"

"For I know the plans I have for you, declares the Lord, plans to prosper you and not to harm you, plans to give you hope and a future."
- Jeremiah 29:11

God's hand is again very apparent in my life. I am growing and becoming the man of His plan. Today I am approached by the YMCA Public Relations and marketing departments to be the anchor speaker at their annual campaign kickoff for the 2014 Turkey Trot.

I am flattered and honored as well as a bit apprehensive about this. My doubts and insecurities kick in. "I am just a legless man from Fort Worth. Why would they pick me to do this?" As I feel myself spiraling out of control, I realize that all I need to do is place my trust in God and everything will work out. God brought me to this, and He will bring me through it.

The day of the event, I arrive early at the venue so that I can get a feel for the energy and space. I anticipate a large, expansive venue but instead find a smaller "pop-up"-type venue with a very small stage and podium.

My confidence takes a brief hit as I must now process how exactly I am to get to and from the podium on my prosthetic legs.

The event begins and the anxiety builds inside of me. My name is called and I carefully stand and walk up the stairs to the podium. The lights are shining brightly in my face and I see only the lights and the black behind them. I can see no one in the audience. I suddenly feel all alone and that this is just a big joke, I wonder if I have been asked here for someone's twisted amusement. "Is anyone really out there?" I wonder. I compose myself, take a deep breath and begin speaking. I almost inadvertently say something amusing and I hear the laughter from the audience. Ah, so there are people out there! People did show up to hear me! That small amount of laughter connects me to the crowd and I begin comfortably giving my talk. This is the first time I have actually stood in front of a very large group of people to tell my story.

I finish to thunderous applause and I gingerly return to my seat. As the meeting ends, people walk up to me and I receive a multitude of "Attaboys" and many who say, "Keep it up! You're doing a great job. You have an amazing story!"

It is a high similar to what I experience at the end of 5K races.

As the crowd thins, I again sit down and a new feeling sweeps over me. I realize, "I am going to be alright. I don't yet know how or what will happen, but I know my life will be alright. I can make it! I've got this!"

My long-held worries about who would want a man with no legs changes slightly. I now have this feeling inside of me, "Who wouldn't want me?"

With this newly found burst of confidence, I return to training for that very race I have just promoted. Instead of the 5K, I decide to push myself further and sign up for the 10K race. As I return to the gym to train, I realize that I do not really know how to alter my training schedule for the longer race, so I continue training for a 5K. This leads me, one day, to try walking a 10K distance on the treadmill by walking two 5Ks back-to-back. I foolishly begin this exercise with no additional hydration or food.

When I finish, I get off the treadmill and feel a bit cramped, but I also feel confident that I can complete the race.

Although I feel well, I apparently look a little pale because one of the staff members looks at me and says, "Are you ok?" I tell her I just finished a 10K and she says, "You don't look well at all. Just sit down and let me get you something to drink."

After a couple of bottles of water and two protein bars, I look and feel well enough to go home. I also feel confident about the upcoming race. One thing special about this race is that I will be joined by three other amputees, two of them doing the 10K with me and the other doing the 5K.

The day of the race, while walking to the starting line, I run into my old friend Renee, my bathroom buddy from a prior race. She enthusiastically tells me that once she finishes the race, she will get some water and food and then come back to meet my team and walk with us to the finish line.

As usual, we are all at the very back of the pack of runners. One change to my racing uniform is our shirts which have been provided by Joey. On the front is the Cheldan Homes logo along with other marketing information but on the back, it is emblazoned with TEAM NORCOTT! So, those of us in the back of the race are all wearing these t-shirts.

Around the mile four marker, Renee meets up with Team Norcott and begins walking with us.

As is often the case, the last runners are followed by a police escort. Somewhere around the three to four-mile mark, the officer drives off in his truck for a short while. When he returns to his position behind us, he gets on his PA and says, "Mr. Norcott, Mr. Norcott? My wife knows you." I have a brief moment of concern, wondering, "Is this good or bad?" The officer then pulls up beside me and asks, "Mr. Norcott, do you remember Kat Steiger?" I think back and remember that Kat was hired at MedStar in 1997 about the same time I was hired. While the officer was taking his break, his wife called asking what was taking him so long to come home. He told her that there were a few amputees in the race, walking slowly, and it was taking longer than usual. He must have also mentioned Team Norcott because it triggered her memory and our working together many years earlier.

A couple of intersections later as I walk by his truck, I ask him, "At the end of the race, would you mind taking a couple of pictures with me?" He looks at me a moment and says, "I thought you would never ask."

We take many pictures of Team Norcott along with our new friend, the police officer.

"I did it!" I rejoice, "I completed 6.2 miles."

In spite of my troubles at home, I feel a new confidence in me and, for the first time, I can see a new horizon in my life. "There is a place in this world for David Norcott. There are things I can accomplish and make manifest. The fact that I have no legs does not limit me, only my thoughts limit me."

Unlike my early races, I leave this race feeling physically strong and emotionally confident. Driving home I decided to celebrate by stopping at a local Whataburger. As I approach the restaurant, I start experiencing roaming cramps throughout my body. Interestingly it starts as a phantom cramp in my non-existent foot and works its way up to my thighs, then my butt, my back and on up to my neck and arms.

I enjoy my burger and head home. Later in the day I join my friend Libbey and her mother for Thanksgiving dinner. At the end of the meal, just before dessert, I can barely keep my eyes open. I am far more exhausted than I realize. Libbey looks at me and says, "David, why don't you just go home and get some sleep?"

As we enter December, I realize that I really want to spend this holiday season with Kyle, I really want to establish some traditions and memories, but it is best for me to leave things alone. So, once again, I have a quiet birthday and Christmas dinner and I pray for my son and my relationships with both him and his sister.

CHAPTER 24:

I've Got This!

It is that time of year when I regularly visit my Primary Care Physician (PCP). I usually see her about once a year, sometimes twice. She has been my doctor since Lecia and I were married. She is a warm, loving person and I trust her completely.

While talking to her, she again brings up a rather sore point between us. She asks me, "David, I really want you to reconsider getting a service dog. I have patients who have them and don't really need or use them. You, on the other hand, are the perfect candidate and would benefit tremendously from the help and companionship these dogs provide!"

She has been giving me this same speech for about four years now. I squirm slightly in my chair and give her the same answer as each time before, "No! I have been breaking free from all of the support I have needed in the past, I have been breaking free from my dependencies. Why do you want me to have another crutch in my life? Don't you realize that I want to be an elite prosthetic user like the athletes I admire?"

When I get out to my car her question still burns inside of me. I curse loudly at this woman I care so much about as I drive away from her office. Why does she keep bringing this up? Why won't she listen to me? I know she cares for me and has my best interest at heart, but here she goes yet again about this service dog. I want to stand on my own, be my own man. I don't need the responsibilities and costs associated with a dog.

It is now January of 2015. As is part of my routine, I attend a meeting of the Dallas Support Group. While there, a good friend and father figure comes over to me. Gary Scott and his wife Jeanna are two very dear friends of mine and Gary catches me off guard with his question, "David, do you trust me?" I feel and probably look quite confused as I answer, "Of course I trust you, Gary."

Gary shows me a website for *Discovery Dallas* Training. The website says that it is a personal development conference. I'm not sure what this is all about, but I do trust Gary and Jeanna and I can see the excitement in their eyes. So, I tentatively agree.

When I get home, I return to the website to see what additional information I can find. What I discover is that there *is* no additional information, hence, my need to simply trust Gary.

I approach my regular running buddy and fellow amputee Larry Olchak about this training and ask if he would also be interested in going. Larry was with me in both the May 2014 5K race and the 10K Turkey Trot. He looks things over and decides that he will go as well.

So, we both register for this mystery course. I tell Gary that I have registered and his only advice to me is to "Work Hard."

The seminar/conference is held at the Crowne Plaza Hotel. I enter the lobby of the hotel and see many people in business dress milling around. I cannot help but wonder what exactly I have gotten myself into.

What does happen in that room cannot fully be discussed. It is brutal, deep, emotional work. I exit the first weekend with my "Contract." My contract states that I am a "Powerful and Loving Man." Hmm.... Sounds good to me! It is not exactly how this legless man has seen himself in the past, but it is a moniker with which I think I can live and aspire to be.

Through *Discovery Dallas* I am finally able to set down some very heavy baggage I have been carrying with me. I am able to finally admit that I was not only emotionally and physically abused as a child, I was also sexually abused from about the time I was seven years old.

The moment it came out of my mouth, it no longer had authority over me. The thought doesn't upset me any longer, and it no longer controls me.

What was so interesting about the acceptance is that it finally dawned on me that for it to have happened to me it also had to have happened to my abuser.

The seminar takes place over three weekends which means I will complete the program in April. During the final weekend, my "Mission" in life is formulated. The raw version of my mission is, "To teach young boys how to become men and to teach broken men how to become whole by sharing my heart and my story."

"It is easier to build strong children than to repair broken men." – *Frederick Douglas*

How exactly I am going to "share my story," I do not yet know. But I walk out of the conference confident. I am confident that if I remain focused on God's plan for me and the path He has laid, He will bring the people into my life who are necessary for me to make that mission manifest.

With this newly found desire to share my story with others, I talk to a friend who suggests I join *Toastmasters*. I ponder this suggestion and while at church on Sunday I tell this to a woman I admire. She looks at me and says, "David, you don't need *Toastmasters*. I want you to go home today and get down on your knees. I want you to pray to

God to bring you the audience and the words. I want you to tell God that you want to work for Him."

Her conviction and encouragement cause me to do exactly as she says. I go home and awkwardly kneel down beside my bed on my prosthetic knees. I pray exactly as instructed.

Well, it doesn't take long for God to begin bringing various people into my life. While still at the conference, someone gives me a most amazing book, *The Alchemist* by Paulo Coelho. What a powerful book! It is a book I can recommend to almost everyone. It seems to reflect my own sense of life. I can see my ultimate goal even though I may not always be able to see my path to that goal.

In reading this book, I am reminded of St. Paul in the New Testament of The Bible. Paul wanted to spread the word of Christ through Asia. God had other plans and first sent him to Europe. Paul did eventually get his wish and ministered through Asia, but he was able to take the lessons learned in Europe with him to Asia and was a more effective missionary because of it.

I do know that patience is a virtue; now I need to cement that patience and my trust in God's plan within me.

At work, Joey invites me out to lunch, a rather uncommon occurrence. In the midst of the meal, he shows me an e-mail forwarded to him from a good friend. Embedded in the e-mail is the original message from a young man who is at the end of his rope. He is still living in his trailer home, but it is in foreclosure and his power is about to be shut off. This man reached out to this mutual friend for help. After I read the message, Joey looks at me and says, "David, I do not have an answer for this man, but I know that you do. I know that *you* are the one man I know who has made one positive choice in life and then followed that with another and yet another. You struggled for years, but you kept making good choices. I am confident that you are the answer to this man's problems. If you are willing, we can leave from lunch and go directly to this man's home."

Wow, what am I supposed to say to that except, "Of course!"

We drive onto his property and to his trailer. He comes out wearing sun glasses. As we sit in his shaded yard and talk, I finally say to him, "You need to take those sunglasses off if you want me to talk to you. I need to see your eyes."

He takes off the glasses and tells me how he is struggling with absolutely everything. He relates that when he retrieves his mail at the box by the road, he gets into his car and drives out to it.

His spirit is blue and everything about him is defeated. First, I briefly tell him my story and then I look directly into his eyes and say, "Dude, you need to walk to your mailbox. You need to get your blood moving. I want you to go into your home and open your curtains, bringing light into your now dark home. Every day, I want you to come outside and sit in the sun."

This is my first speaking engagement and it is the first of many more. As the year progresses, I am approached by both my church and the YMCA to speak to other groups.

One of the elements of *Discovery* is called the Service Walk. We are instructed to give back to our community. In addition to my speaking, I look into programs where I might be able to help and I find the organization *Tango Tab*. This organization meets to make sandwiches for the homeless. In working with *Tango Tab*, God opens various doors for me at which to speak and share my story. These venues include a prison, a rehab facility, a children's church, and many more.

Again, I come home at night and bask in that same feeling I had after the YMCA Turkey Trot Kickoff. "I've got this. I can make it!"

God continues bringing people into my life who invite me to speak and inspire others.

I continue training for various races and my calendar begins filling up for the spring/summer/fall seasons.

I get so involved and so excited that I sign up for five races in a single weekend. Two of the races are virtual, meaning there is no actual prescribed course, you run the race on your own time and schedule. The other three are held on Friday night, Saturday morning and then Saturday evening. One of the races is rained out, but I finish the other four.

I feel a tremendous sense of accomplishment in being in these various races and have a similar sense of satisfaction in the time I spend volunteering.

With these various races behind me, I look toward my next challenge and decide that I will tackle a half marathon in early November 2015.

With the fall of 2015 upon me, I am training for the half marathon when I receive a surprising text on my phone. It is from my son, Kyle. He tells me that he would like to come over and pick up his last few possessions still at my home. In the past I tried to make this happen, but would always ask him to meet me at a public place, somewhere I felt safe and certain that things would not escalate. But he never took me up on those past offers.

So, what am I to do? I decide to agree to his coming to my apartment and I then ask a few of my friends to come over as well. Kyle mentioned that he is bringing along a friend of his to help. I feel that having a few of my own friends present will provide both witnesses and possibly "security," if necessary, for me.

As is often true of "The best laid plans" all of my friends are forced to cancel on me at the last minute. Kyle and his friend do come over. I am extremely nervous and cautious as they enter my apartment. As they walk in, neither of them says a word to me. Kyle simply places his phone and keys to my apartment on the front table. They both then walk over to the closet to two bags containing Kyle's possessions. They pick them up and leave.

I am both relieved and sad. I still care so much for my son, but I also know that I did the right thing. I pray for his success and fulfillment in life and that one day we will be reunited in a loving relationship.

Over time I do learn, through social media, that Kyle graduated from Le Cordon Bleu and for that I am very grateful.

I continue my training for the upcoming half marathon. In the midst of everything else, I am approached to help support a new amputee group forming in South Texas. It is just one more of my many volunteer opportunities that lead me into November and my first half marathon!

Yet another blessing and surprise enters my life! During the summer, I am contacted by Scott Eder of Team Cambridge of Dallas. He tells me he has been following me on the racing circuit and he invites me to join Team Cambridge. He would like me to train for a triathlon. WHAT? ME? You've been following ME? I would probably laugh at his offer if I wasn't so overwhelmed with gratitude and pride.

I decide that this is an offer I cannot refuse and I accept. I retire my Team Norcott t-shirts and begin wearing Team Cambridge at my various races.

Also, during this year, I join the Cox Running Club in Fort Worth. During one of the races of the summer season, I meet a wonderful woman, Nurit Garcia, along a trail. I tell her that I am planning on running the half marathon in November and she gives me a blessing, "I tell you what, I'll pace you for that race."

She is not the only one who bestows blessing upon me. As other members of the running club hear about my upcoming race, interest and excitement build. I'm not sure what exactly will happen that day, but I sense something quite amazing.

The night before the race I get an unexpected call from Rhonda Smith, a member of both the Benbrook YMCA and the Cox Running Club. I have briefly met Rhonda, but do not know her well. She tells me that Nurit unexpectedly had to attend a wedding in Las Vegas. Nurit will be flying in on the red-eye flight from Las Vegas but is not sure she can get to the race venue on time to walk with me. Rhonda lovingly offers to meet me there and walk with me if Nurit is late. I discover that Rhonda got my number from the race director, Steve Looney. This group is one of the most supportive to which I have ever belonged since the Fire Departments and Paramedic Services. They accepted me as I am and have helped me grow.

Steve, the race director, asks me to start the race, not with the half-marathon group but with the marathon group instead. This means I will start earlier, hopefully ensuring that I will complete the race with everyone else.

Moments before the gun is fired to start the race, Nurit arrives and enthusiastically joins me on the start line. BAM! And off we go!

Along almost all race routes are "cheerleaders," people encouraging you to continue on. Normally, I find them amusing, but today, I find them annoying. I know about how far I still must walk and when I hear someone yell out to me, "You're almost there! You can do it!" I think, "NO! I am *NOT* almost there! Now hush up and leave me alone!"

About seven hours after starting the race, I re-enter Trinity Park and see the finish line in the near distance (up yonder, for you fellow Texans).

As I approach the arch, I see all of my fellow runners, men and women who finished their races much earlier in the day, all standing there waiting for me and cheering me on. As I get close to the arch, many of them run out to meet me and walk the final length to the finish.

As I step across the finish line with tears running down my cheeks, people run to me with water and snacks. Steve and the Cox brothers are there to congratulate me and they all go above and beyond to recognize my achievement. I am both thrilled and a little embarrassed. I am also thankful for having so many loving people in my life. Emotionally, this is a huge experience. It is like reaching the top of Mt. Everest to me.

Steve gives me various medals, crowning me as if I am an Olympic Champion. I return home with a tremendous amount of memorabilia. It is truly a day I will never forget.

Before heading home, Nurit and I decide to celebrate with lunch. I am ravenous and no amount of food seems able to sate me. I eat and eat and *finally* feel full.

Once home, I am somewhat afraid of removing my prosthetic legs. I know that my stumps are likely to swell from the beating they have just taken. Once swollen, I will be unable to put the legs back on again.

I try to head off the problem and I draw a warm bath, emptying a bag of Epsom salts into the water. I crawl in and soak for a very long time, reveling in my latest accomplishment. It is rather difficult to explain, but I surprisingly feel both full and empty at the same time.

Within those conflicting feelings, I smile and again think, "I've got this!"

It is only 6pm, and I am so tired I decide to just crawl into bed early. My body is tired and my energy is fully spent.

My body is not fully recovered, but work is there on Monday. I arrive at the office and basically just waddle around as I am too sore to walk properly. No matter, I hold it as a badge of accomplishment for all to see. I now quickly own my racing accomplishments; no longer do I need time to let them percolate into me to fully accept it. I embrace my new life and my new outlook and am thankful and joyous.

With this latest accomplishment, I surprise even myself by entering this year's YMCA Turkey Trot in the 5K category. The Turkey Trot is less than 30 days after the half marathon.

I close out 2015 having been in a total of 33 races. Not one to rest on my laurels, on New Year's Eve, Larry and I run back-to-back 5Ks: One race on New Year's Eve Day and the other on January 1, 2016. It is a great way to usher in the New Year and my new life.

Great things *MUST* be ahead in 2016!

CHAPTER 25:
Someone To Watch Over Me

As 2016 begins, I remain involved with *Discovery* and, as an alumnus, am invited in February to be what is called a cheerleader, encouraging those attending for the first time.

While standing there, an amazing, Divine event happens. A man entering the lobby notices my prosthetic legs and enthusiastically approaches me. He introduces himself as Andreas Schultz and tells me that he is the Chief Financial Officer (CFO) of Otto Bock. Otto Bock is the company which makes the computer-controlled knees in my legs.

Mr. Schultz tells me that he has never actually seen an amputee out in the world using his company's equipment.

Mr. Schultz cannot stop smiling or shaking my hand. His elation and excitement seem a bit exaggerated, but I also feel that the meeting is about more than just my knees. We are supposed to meet; it is yet another divinely orchestrated event in my life.

I fulfill yet another goal in my new life. I finally pay off all of my various debts. I tell Joey of my accomplishment and he suggests taking each of my final bills, the ones showing a now zero balance, and putting them all into a scrap book to remind me of this accomplishment.

I have been supporting Get Your Limb on Amputee Support Group in Sequin, South Texas and I receive a call from David Richie.

David owns two prosthetic offices in the area and has decided to consolidate the two into one new office complex. The building is complete and he will be holding an Open House for the new office on Sunday. He invites many of his patients and asks if I can also attend.

I drive down on Wednesday night, after work, and meet David at his home. It is late and David prepares dinner for me. I now travel without my power chair, taking only my prosthetic legs. We have a pleasant evening together and I retire to bed.

The next morning, we drive to his beautiful new offices in New Braunsfel, Texas. Many people attend the event and many pictures are taken. I move through the crowd welcoming and meeting as many people as I can. They are all warm and wonderful and I am thrilled that I made the trip from my home.

As much as I would like to stay, I look at the clock and consider the 3 ½ hour drive still ahead of my return home to Fort Worth. I also have to work in the morning, need sleep, and I need time for my legs to recharge.

On the way home, my drive turns into a nightmare as traffic comes to a complete stop about 10pm near the city of Temple. All of the lanes are closed for construction and all traffic must be diverted off the highway and onto surface streets.

I am upset and frustrated but there is nothing I can do except patiently wait it out. I do not get home until 4:30am on Friday morning. Once in my apartment, I immediately take off my legs and start charging them. I then go in and take a shower.

There is really no time for me to sleep before work. I eat a light breakfast, pour myself some strong coffee and check my legs. They are still not fully charged, but I am out of time. I do not want to be late for work.

I put on my legs, pour a to-go cup of coffee and head for the office.

As I sit at the desk this morning, I am keenly aware of a shift in the office energy. I notice various employees entering the conference room with Joey; when they exit, most are in tears.

I am physically exhausted and between my PTSD and my lack of sleep I become quite anxious. I am on edge because I cannot understand what is happening.

I finally tell myself to just look down and focus on my own job. I tell myself, "Don't look toward the conference room. "

After lunch, I feel a bit more relaxed and return to my desk. I am just getting comfortable when Joey steps out of his office and says, "David, can you please come in here?"

I waddle into his office and then notice Kelly, from HR, entering as well. My heart rate increases, I feel my body getting warm, and my anxieties quickly return.

Joey looks at me and says, "David, you have exceeded all of my expectations and you have reached the point where you have outgrown Cheldan Homes. Unfortunately, I have to lay you off. Relax, though. I may no longer be your employer, but I am still your friend and I will continue being a mentor to you if you choose." Even though I am only a part-time employee, Joey presents me with a generous severance package and says, "This week, I want you to go to a park, someplace peaceful. I want you to sit back and dream. I don't want you to worry about anything. This is all going to work out as God has planned. I want you to sit back and imagine what it is going to be like for you to stand in front of a crowd of 20,000 people and inspire them to do more and to be more."

I am speechless, but I trust Joey and I simply nod in assent.

The housing market has changed and so must Cheldan Homes. Joey is scaling back and I know I am not critical to the operation.

Logically I know this must happen, but working for Joey has also been a great comfort for me.

Kelly gives me some paperwork to sign and I am escorted back to my desk to gather my things.

I leave the building with my heart sinking deep into my stomach over the concern of the unknown. I remind myself that six years earlier, I was merely a pitiful legless man sitting on the floor at the gas station with no hope for my future. Twelve years before that, I was lying dead on the pavement in Fort Worth. Now, in spite of what has just happened, I'm leaving on good terms. Like my driving trip to Maryland and Pennsylvania, Joey has again assured me that he has my back. No matter what, he is my friend and he will help me.

As I focus on all the good that has happened in my life, I know I can trust both Joey and God that this is merely the beginning of my journey. There is more ahead for Joseph David Norcott, Jr. although it may not be obvious at this moment. I decide to view this day as a promotion, a day that Joey has simply pushed me out of the nest so that I can fly on my own.

I do as Joey instructed and two days later drive to Trinity Park, the site of many of my racing accomplishments. I sit there in peace and contemplate how everything in life is interconnected. As much as I try to think positive thoughts, the doubt keeps bubbling up and I think, "Uh oh, now what am I going to do?" Yet, I also am reminded just how far I have come in these last 18 years and how much I have overcome. "I survived an accident that should have killed me, certainly I can survive this!"

I relax again and begin to pray. I know that if I simply surrender to God and His will, His plan will be made manifest in my life. I keep reciting Psalms 46:10 over and over in my mind, "Be still and know that I am God." I can almost hear God saying to me, "Let go child. Do not try controlling what is about to happen."

In April, I am invited to volunteer at the YMCA for Kid's Day. While at the event, I am approached by two of the staff members of the "Y" and they offer me a job. They tell me that they will e-mail me an application. Once back at home, I complete the forms, return them and am informed that I am hired. I am given the title of Wellness Coach. I do some online training and begin working at the YMCA to help others as I have been helped. I sit back and bask in the realization that everything truly is working out. I am good.

With everything that has happened this year, I am not racing as much as before and I decide to sign up for the Trinity 5000 Summer Series this summer.

At one race, I am approached by H.B. Wise of Movin' Pictures. I have met and talked to him several times before and he has some ideas to interview me for a series of podcasts he would like to produce. Toward the end of the conversation, he tells me that he has a friend he would also like me to meet and asks if I am open to lunch in the near future.

A date is set and I wait to learn what else God has in store for me.

The day arrives and I rendezvous with HB at a race site in Fort Worth. He introduces me to Tom Martin and we drive over to the Stockyards for lunch. As we sit there, several people I know from various races also enter and greet me.

As we talk, Tom tells me of his health challenges and that he has written his autobiography. He also tells me that he volunteers for Canine Companions for Independence (CCI) and casually asks me, "David, have you ever considered getting a service dog?" I pause and think, "Jeez, now I not only have my doctor harping at me about this, now *this* guy is saying the same thing." Unable to catch myself, I respond with an overly firm "NO! I am not really interested in a service dog, but thank you."

Tom hands me his business card and says, "If you would like any help with your biography, please call or e-mail me. If you change your mind about the dog, I'd be happy to help you with that as well."

A week or so later I receive a call at home from Tom inviting me to lunch. We meet and I wonder about the purpose of this meeting. I ask how I can help him and he looks almost confused. He then offers his help for my book and asks if I might like to visit his Lions Club meeting the following week.

I know little about Lions Club but dinner is served and that convinces me to attend. Right now, my schedule is quite flexible and I am usually very food-motivated.

Upon entering the restaurant, Tom introduces me to Steve Blackman and his service dog Gottlieb. Over dinner, Steve tells of his time in the US Army as an elite combat soldier. Back home, he was in a training accident that radically changed his life, forcing him to retire from the Army. Like me, Steve suffered a traumatic brain injury and continues battling PTSD. With so much in common, I approach Steve after dinner and talk to him more about CCI and his service dog. I express my concerns about becoming dependent upon a dog and that I see this as a step backward rather than as an asset to me. Steve redirects my focus and tells me how a service dog can improve my life.

I leave the restaurant with a completely different perspective. Once I am home, I log onto the CCI website and read more about the organization. I find the link for those interested in their dogs and answer a few simple questions. The site then tells me that they will mail me an application.

The next morning, I text Tom and tell him what I have done. He texts back that he is sitting on his couch and sobbing with joy.

A few days later I receive a surprisingly large packet of information and paperwork from CCI. The application process is even more involved than when I applied for work with the Washington D.C. fire department!

In the packet they ask for various references from doctors and physical therapists.

Around this time, I happen to have my regular appointment with my doctor. As I sit in the examination room, she enters. With her back to me I say, "Hey, you know this service dog you keep encouraging me to get? Are you really going to help me?"

She spins around and is smiling from ear to ear. It isn't just her face that is smiling, it is also her heart. "What changed your mind?"

I smile back and say, "I just needed some extra help. God brought some other people into my life that helped me understand how a service dog can benefit me." I then tell her about my conversation with Steve Blackman.

She looks directly at me and says, "Absolutely! You get started and I will do whatever is necessary to help you."

The application also asks me to list out my daily tasks and lifestyle, taking pictures of my home and work environments. It takes me time to list all of the various things I do in a week and I become overzealous with my photographs.

When it comes time to e-mail the pictures, I find I must severely limit the number I can actually send to them.

Now that everything is submitted, there is really little I can do but sit back and wait.

Even though I have worked at the YMCA such a short time, my supervisor asks me if I would like to become a Personal Trainer. I go through the training and receive my certification.

Leaving work one evening, as I am approaching my car, a man comes rushing over to me. The Westside YMCA is not in the best area of town and I am somewhat concerned for my safety. As he gets closer to me, he says, "I don't want to hurt you, I just want to ask you about your prosthetic legs."

He tells me that his son is an amputee from birth. Since I am standing next to my car, I show him the hand controls that allow me to drive. As we are about to depart, I tell him to invite his son to come down to the Westside YMCA so that we can meet. I give him my card and ask that his son call me.

The man seems very happy that he was able to meet me.

In November, Tom calls and invites me to attend a graduation ceremony at the local CCI regional facility. I don't really know what this is all about, but Tom is very enthusiastic and I decide to tag along.

As we sit in this rather large room, I see Steve Blackman standing along the side with Gottlieb. We go over and speak to him briefly. The room fills with many of the volunteers, including people who are puppy raisers and their puppies.

During the ceremony, the current graduates are matched with their dogs. As this happens, Tom nudges me and says, "Very soon, that will be you up there."

I'm slightly irritated and think, "Hey, I've not yet even been interviewed. Don't jinx the process!"

A few days later, I am in the midst of my morning routine when my phone rings. Something about this call causes my heart to race a bit as I reach for the phone.

The woman on the other end says, "This is CCI and we would like to invite you in for a face-to-face interview," after hanging up the phone I immediately text Tom to keep him abreast of my progress.

As I enter December, I find myself in the worst TBI struggles and PTSD storm I have experienced since the accident. I can barely get out of bed each morning.

One day, I am so frustrated that I call my father. I tell him what I am experiencing and he says, "You are going to waste a lot of time and energy worrying about how things will turn out, worrying about things you cannot control. The only thing you can control is you. If you are not careful, you will manifest all that worries you and what you fear."

I hang up and pull myself together. I shower, dress, and head to work at the Benbrook YMCA. When I arrive, I ask my boss if we can talk. I tell her about my situation, about my PTSD storm. She looks at me lovingly and says, "Whatever you need, we are here to help you."

"What?" I think, "Are you kidding?"

She then says, "We need you here. We need all of you here."

In spite of all the wonderful things that have happened in my life and all of the wonderful people I have met, I am still surprised by this response. I think, "I have just asked for help from my employer and she gives abundantly to me."

Divinely, all of my appointments cancel for that night and I am able to quietly work with others.

Driving home after work, I notice that my gas tank is about half full. I briefly think about stopping for gas and then change my mind. What I really want to do is just get home and relax. As I approach the turn for the station, something tells me to turn in anyway.

I always pay for my gas at the pump, never entering the store itself. This time, with His hand guiding me, I walk into the store. I discover that no one is at the counter. Surprised, I saunter around the store wondering where the clerk might have gone. Just about then, a young girl emerges from the back with a cell phone pressed against her ear.

She is clearly overwhelmed with emotions from the call. When she sees me, she apologizes profusely for making me wait. She positions herself behind the counter and I reach out my hand to her, "Hi, my name is David. May I pray for you?"

She completely loses control of herself in tears. She sets the phone down and tells me, "I just got a call from my family in California. My sister was in a drive-by shooting several days ago and has been on life support. I was just told that she is doing so well that they will be taking her off the support machines. My concern is that my sister will go back to the lifestyle that put her in the hospital this time."

We pray together and I can see and feel the stress fall from her. I look up and ask, "Can I give you a hug?" She cannot get around the counter fast enough and I embrace her with a strong, loving, long hug.

I walk out to my car and drive off without getting any gas.

Arriving home, I reflect on many of the stories in the Bible. I consider how God uses people when they are at the worst point in their lives and asks them to minister to others. I realize how important it is for one broken person to minister to another.

I review this day in my mind. It was a day I did not want to even get out of bed, I did not want to get up, dress up, or show up. I yielded to God and called my father for help. When I asked for help at work I was abundantly rewarded with compassion, support, and understanding.

Following God's lead, I turned into the gas station so that I could meet this young girl in need.

In the midst of one of my biggest storms, I am led to meet a girl in the middle of even a bigger storm.

The day of my face-to-face interview at CCI arrives. The interview is dynamic, interactive, and quite interesting. They first have me interact with a dog-like prop and then they bring in this magnificent, huge, black Labrador named Chase, a big, masculine, alpha-type dog. My heart melts as I reach out to pet Chase. I briefly wonder, "Could this actually be my dog?"

During the interview, the staff tells me of many of the tasks the dog can perform for me, many of which I have never suspected or considered.

In spite of all of my emotions that are poured into this interview, it ends on a rather sterile note. They all stand, look at me and say, "Thank you for coming in and meeting with us. We will send you an answer by mail."

As I dejectedly walk to my car I think, "Six months of paperwork and referrals and I'm just casually dismissed from the room? Really?"

On my way back to my car, I walk past the room where the graduation ceremony had been held just one month before. My mind can't help rewinding back to Tom's nudge and comment. For a brief moment I think, "Did Tom really jinx this for me? Is this all his fault?"

Over the weekend I go to church and then on Monday back to work. Tuesday morning, I am up early and in the midst of my morning routine of meditation when the phone rings. I don't usually take any calls during that time, but I am once again led to stop what I am doing and answer.

"Good morning!" says the lovely voice on the other end. "This is Maria at CCI. We have a couple of dogs here that might meet your needs and we would like to invite you to be a part of the January training class."

I sit back in total shock and then begin screaming like a school girl. The entire world has just been handed to me!

I breathlessly reply, "Of course! Of course, I will be there!"

My brain quickly kicks in and I add, "Oh, wait, I really need to check with work first. I need to make sure that I can have the time off."

I immediately e-mail my supervisor at the YMCA and her reply is swift. "Um, YES! Of course, you can have the time off!"

I call Maria back and let her know that I am a go for January. She tells me that I will receive a formal acceptance letter and a packet of information to review prior to the class.

With all of the really important stuff out of the way, I then text Tom and let him know what has happened. I also privately forgive him for his comments the month before.

Within a few days I receive a rather large packet from CCI in the mail. Within it is a guide that I am asked to read at least once before attending class. I pore through all of the material and come across a statement that makes me pause, "Do not attach to specific dogs during the first few days of class. Please trust the process."

I realize that emotionally, I have already bonded to Chase. My heart falls briefly as I know I must let him go and be open to what lies ahead for me.

The CCI campus is only 50 miles from my home. I am given the option of either living on campus for the two-week training or commuting to and from my home. I decide it is better for me to live on campus so that I can completely focus my attention on the course work.

On the first two days, we are introduced to various dogs and permitted to interact with them. I write down the names of all of the dogs and instinctively circle the names of two of them, Chase, my big buddy from the interview, and Kinsey. Next to Kinsey's name I write, "I liked."

The course work is almost overwhelming and I am thankful I decided to remain on campus. In this way I can completely immerse myself in the work and not think about the daily commute.

The day of the pre-match comes. I watch as dogs are led into the room on their leashes and the leash turned over to each student. I impatiently wait my turn to discover which dog the staff has decided is best for me.

I am sitting in a chair when this beautiful, small, female, yellow Labrador retriever is brought through the door. I know she is for me and I feel a lump in my throat. It is Kinsey. I am handed her leash and am unsure of what exactly to do. I follow the lead of others in the room and get down on the floor with her, lavishing her with love and attention.

In spite of everything good that has happened in my life, in this moment that terrible tape begins replaying in my head, "You are not worthy of this. You are not good enough." I am still filled with doubts, fears, and insecurities.

As I hug her, Kinsey gently licks my face. Kinsey lets me know that I am worthy, that I am good enough.

As we all sit around talking about this match, we are asked to give our dogs basic commands to see how they respond to us. Kinsey obediently listens to me. When I sit down again, I feel a slight tug on my prosthetic leg at my stump. I look down to the floor and see Kinsey's head resting on my shoes.

In that moment, in my heart, I know, "This is my girl."

Our first night together goes smoothly, but in the middle of the second night, Kinsey begins whining and is clearly distressed. At first, my brain is not sure what I am hearing and I wake confused. After a couple of moments, I get up out of my bed and shuffle over to her kennel. I can see and feel that something is quite wrong. I crawl along the floor and take her out behind the patio of my room. Poor Kinsey has a massive case of diarrhea. Once she finishes, we go back into our room and I settle back into bed.

The drama is not over though. This same scenario plays out several more times. I frantically text one of the staff telling her what is happening and say, "I think I broke Kinsey."

But I receive no reply that night.

In the morning, I rise and prepare myself for the day ahead. As we all assemble for breakfast, we are asked about our second night with our new friends. I explain what happened that night and am told, "She probably just has a case of 'stress stomach.' Keep in mind that in the last few months she has gone from her puppy raiser's home to the kennels here on campus for advanced training and now she is with you in a new kennel in your room. This is not unusual and she will probably be fine going forward."

Sunday, we have the day free. I am exhausted from all of the work and decide to just stay in my room and relax. I do not have television at home, so it is a treat to just lounge in bed with Kinsey, watch some television, and nap. In every moment I find myself more in love with this little girl.

One day at lunch, a lunch provided by a local Lions Club, Tom comes for a visit. While there, I get to show him around the various parts of the campus he has not previously seen, including my room. He is busily taking pictures of everything. He then gets to meet Kinsey as well. Tom is a total dog-person and the two of them quickly became fast friends.

As Friday and graduation approaches, we are told that one of the events of the day is breakfast at a local country club. We are permitted to invite one or two friends. I call Tom and another friend of mine to join me. After breakfast, we will all return to the CCI campus for the ceremony itself.

Also attending the breakfast are the puppy raisers of the various dogs which are graduating. I am introduced to the couple who raised and trained Kinsey. I learn they have raised many puppies for CCI. Kinsey is thrilled to see them and I am happy that they can spend some time with her as well.

Back on campus I walk into the same room where just three months earlier I sat with Tom watching other graduates. I see many members of Tom's Lions Club who are there to support me. Tom also introduces me to two Lions District dignitaries he invited to the graduation. He wanted to introduce them to me as well as to this wonderful organization.

After the ceremony, we all step outside for many pictures.

In spite of this being such a joyful day and seeing so many people who are in the room to support me, I can still hear those upsetting words in my head, "You are not worthy of all of this."

About two weeks after the graduation ceremony, Tom calls and asks to meet with me. There is excitement in his voice as he tells me he has a gift for me.

The three of us meet at a local restaurant and Tom beams as he hands me a wrapped package. I open it and inside is a beautiful printed photo book of my CCI journey. He had taken all of the pictures he took of me, Kinsey, the campus, and graduation and had them printed in this book for me to look back and remember.

A couple of weeks later while at an event with my *Discovery* family, someone turns to me and says, "You know David, you are a man's man." I understood the positive intention in his words, but I honestly was not sure what was meant by them. It was not until I got home that I sat down I researched this phrase.

Puzzled by the explanation, I think, "Really? I am a man people admire? A man they look up to? Is he kidding me?"

I let it all sink in to my mind and my heart. For as unworthy as I have felt most of my life, I suddenly realize and accept that I am truly redeemed. I am the man that God has chiseled and formed. I fully realize that I am enough and that my heart is full.

CHAPTER 26:

An Open Road

Imagine yourself driving rapidly down a four-lane expressway in the far-left lane when suddenly the traffic slows and comes to a complete stop. You continue creeping forward, eventually realizing that this lane must merge right. You eventually discover that all lanes are closed except the far-right lane. Unable to exit the expressway, you are forced to continue in a slow, stop-and-go fashion, trying to patiently await your turn. Over an hour passes before you finally squeeze over and basically crawl the last 1,000 feet. Reaching the cause of the lane closures, you look forward to a road that is wide open. You press down on the accelerator and whip into a new lane. You are free from all of your limitations and everything is now possible.

It is February 14, 2017 and I report to work for the first time with Kinsey at my side. It is Valentine's Day, and Kinsey is definitely, my Valentine!

I first must educate my co-workers about Kinsey, teaching them that Kinsey is not merely a pet, she is my service dog. Therefore, she is not to be petted or even interacted with without my permission. She is on duty while I am at work and in her vest uniform. After receiving permission from me, I give Kinsey the "release" command and she is permitted to be merely a dog again.

I quickly discover the benefits of having Kinsey at work with me at the YMCA, especially when I am with autistic children on the gym floor. Her presence just seems to change everything.

I have to mentally re-work my schedule slightly with Kinsey in my life. She has her own required schedule that must mesh with my own. She has to be taken outside about every four hours. It is not precise timing, but it is something I must constantly keep in mind.

In May 2017 while sitting at a table at the Benbrook YMCA and with a member, I hear a lot of racket behind me. It is the sound of noisemakers and party horns along with a lot of clapping. I quickly turn around and discover that I am being awarded West Side's YMCA "Employee of the Month!"

This award gives me a great deal of satisfaction and joy, being recognized and validated for the work I do here. I cannot help but believe that Kinsey is as much a part of the reasons for the award as me.

With Kinsey in my life, the constant PTSD storm in my head that was always simmering around a level five or six now seems almost imperceptible. Kinsey is not trained to be an emotional support dog, yet her presence has that same effect.

I have taken most of the year off in racing, but in November 2017, I volunteer to help at the Turkey Trot on Thanksgiving morning. After I finish, I pick up Tom and we head to a friend's ranch near Corsicana for an afternoon Thanksgiving dinner. The friend is someone I know from *Discovery*, someone who invites "orphans" over for the big dinner.

They have a beautiful sprawling ranch with a variety of animals. Dinner is held in a building that was likely a large garage at one time. One wall is completely open to the ranch and the weather is perfect. We enjoy a lovely meal and good fellowship; it is something out of a Norman Rockwell painting.

Randy, the owner, knows that I have always wanted to ride a horse and offers to let me do so after dessert. He leads out this absolutely enormous, calm, beautiful horse that he refers to as a "paint horse." At its shoulder, he is much taller than me and I think even taller than Tom (who is six foot six inches). Now, how am I to mount this monster horse? We come up with a plan for me to get onto the bed of Randy's pickup truck and then crawl into the saddle. It works perfectly and off I go across the front lawn area.

After my newest of life's thrills, Randy asks Tom if he would like to ride as well. In spite of Tom's height, he too has to first get into the truck's bed and then seems to uncomfortably straddle the horse and suddenly drop down (painfully, it seems) upon the saddle.

On the ride home Tom tells me that the jeans he is wearing were a bit too tight to easily mount the horse, but once he was in position, felt he could not back down. "I was in a position over the saddle where I could either give up and get off the horse or simply plop down onto the saddle and ride. I could not give up after David had just ridden, so I made the decision to let gravity simply put me in the proper position. Yes, it was painful, but I got to ride the horse."

At the end of January 2018, I am invited to the Employees-of-the-Month luncheon for the twenty-four employees who were employees of the month in 2017 at Benbrook and Westside YMCAs. As they review the various recipients and their accomplishments, I cannot imagine how I can compete with the others and I am shocked when my name is called and am awarded Fitness Department Employee of the Year of the Westside YMCA. I walk to the front of the room and ask the crowd to please cover their ears. After a brief pause, I let out a Tarzan-style victory yell, celebrating my win.

Time moves forward and God continues to bless me with opportunities to help others. In the late spring, the Dallas Amputee

Network offers to sponsor me to attend the Amputee Coalition of America (ACA) Convention 2018, in Tucson, Arizona. I excitedly agree and look forward to the date. This will be the second time Kinsey and I will fly on an airplane together, so that is yet another new experience for the two of us.

The convention is hosted at a beautiful large resort. After checking into my room and putting my things away, I walk down to the lobby and find a seat. I enjoy watching others enter the convention lobby area and I chat with people now and then. Kinsey and I are comfortably sitting in a corner when a woman walks by, pushing a specially-modified stroller. In the stroller is a young, handsome boy with no legs.

As she passes in front of me, the young boy eyes Kinsey. His eyes brighten with joy and his arms reach toward her. The woman stops the stroller and the boy quickly exits and ambles on his stumps over to Kinsey. His smile melts the hearts of everyone around us. He and Kinsey become immediate best friends.

In talking to the woman, she tells me that the boy's name is Noah. I learn that he was born with no legs and that he was abandoned by his birth mother. This woman is not only the nurse who cares for him, but also his foster mother. She has long considered adopting Noah and recently began the process to do so.

Even here at the convention, Noah often plays the helpless child victim card, requesting assistance to do almost everything, yet when he sees Kinsey, he belies his limitations by easily leaving his stroller and walking or crawling to Kinsey. It is almost as if he already has prosthetics.

This all completely fills my heart. I almost do not care if I get anything else out of the convention. It seems that God sent me to this convention specifically to meet Noah. These moments with Noah and Kinsey are pure joy.

I give Noah's mother information on Canine Companions and encourage her to contact them. It seems clear to me that Noah is the perfect candidate for a service dog.

In July 2018 Jenny, a co-worker at the Westside YMCA, comes to me and says, "I have someone here you need to meet."

I walk out into the lobby and there in his wheelchair is this man, about thirty years old and a congenital quadruple amputee. His name is Trenton. With him is his health aide. We talk for a while and I say to him, "Why don't you come back in the morning when I am working on the Fitness floor."

Trenton looks up at me and says, "You know, you've met my dad."

My mind begins racing through the various people I have met and spoken to, but I cannot place who his father might be. I obviously have a very confused look on my face so Trenton smiles and says, "You met him here in the parking lot one night." I then recalled that awkward evening meeting in the lot the prior year with the man who approached me as I was leaving work.

Trenton does come back the next day and we begin working out together. Using a series of exercise "steps" I have Trenton first get out of his chair and onto the floor of the gym. He tells me that he has not been on the floor in almost ten years, that he usually only goes from his chair to the couch or his bed.

We are all surprised at the amount of strength Trenton has. We begin working out with various equipment and medicine balls. We constantly have to increase the weight and number of repetitions he does as he continues to astound us with his strength. It seems that no matter what we give him to do, he can always do more.

Trenton is quite the blessing for me as I can now fully see how I can give to others all that has been given so generously to me.

Now, being able to help and encourage others is filling my days, my heart, and my soul. I can look back at the mistakes I have made in this life and also reflect upon my journey of redemption. By listening to God and following His plan, this is now my life: I get to do all of these things. I get to work for the YMCA, and when there is a person with a physical, emotional, or cognitive challenge, I am the one who usually is called upon to work with them. I was once a man who was angry, rebellious and lazy and now I get to help others find their path.

As I was once told by a friend, "David, you are not just 'enough' you are 'more than enough.'" I hold that quote close to my heart, working to replace all of the negative words in my head with these six words, "David, you are more than enough."

I realize that the road ahead for me is clear and open and that only my mind can limit the endless possibilities.

"Trust in the Lord with all your heart and lean not on your own understanding." – Proverbs 3:5

PART V:
Reflections On David's Journey

CHAPTER 27:

Cecil Bacher

It had been a very long, busy day. As a Paramedic for MedStar, I started my shift at 7am on September 3, 1998, and my partner and I immediately began responding to calls. We had one patient who required CPR, another who suffered a massive stroke, and one who died. Our day started busy and never eased up. Around midnight, I received yet another call directing me to Eagle Mountain to the intersection of Boat Club Road and Ten Mile Bridge Road.

Upon arriving the carnage was terrible, chunks of automobiles were everywhere and there were already many police and fire units on the scene. I got out of my bus and walked over to the barely recognizable car in front of me. I could see the driver trapped, with the engine of the car basically sitting on his lap. While we surveyed the damage, a fire started that we were able to put out with a small extinguisher. After the firefighters extracted the limp body from the wreckage, I was able to begin my work on this badly burned and damaged man.

I looked again into the car and could see a MedStar Uniform in the back. It was then that I realized that this man was one of our own. As I looked further in the car, I found a MedStar badge and learned it was David Norcott. I knew David, but was not close to him. As in any profession, you do your best for everyone, but an extra amount of adrenaline kicks in when you realize you are brothers.

I immediately called for more assistance including air transport from CareFlight. I did my best to care for David and was able to bring him back to life. David's badly damaged body could not comfortably sustain his life and again gave up the fight. After several scenarios of life/death/life/death, I was finally able to stabilize him. About that time the CareFlight crew arrived to pick him up. I asked "To which hospital will you take this patient?" they replied, "Harris Hospital in Fort Worth." I immediately protested, "This man has serious burns and life-threatening injuries. He needs to be at the best trauma and burn center in the area. I want you to transport him to Parkland Hospital in Dallas." At that time, Parkland was well known for their trauma response and team.

As the helicopter lifted off of the ground, I knew that my shift was over. Although not scheduled to finish until 7am, I had nothing left in me to give anyone else. I called my supervisor and told him I was wrapping things up.

I knew that Tony, David's best friend, also worked for MedStar. Over the next several months, Tony kept us all apprised of David's progress at Parkland and the hospitals and rehab facilities following David's time at Parkland.

David pushed the envelope that night and continued pushing the envelope for the next several months at Parkland hospital.

It was several years later when I ran into David at a McDonalds restaurant. David was in a wheelchair and seemed to be doing quite well. We exchanged the usual pleasantries, but I was unable to say much more. The memories and emotions of that night flooded back into my mind and heart and I think I was just unable to speak. There was a lot I likely wanted to say, but no words came out. I could feel tears running down my cheeks as I kept looking at David and thinking how it was a miracle he had even survived.

We should have exchanged phone numbers that day, we probably should have gotten together and talked more about that night, but my mind was not thinking logically, my emotions were in control and I did not do or say all that I should.

I was given another chance a couple of years later when I ran into David at Sam's Club with his fiancé, Lecia. Again, it was wonderful to see him and I was thrilled that he had found someone to love him. Also, with me that day was my fourteen-year-old son, Joshua. David looked at Joshua and said, "You know, your father saved my life."

I think it stunned both Joshua and me. I have never thought of myself as any sort of hero. I just happened to be on call that night and was the one who helped David. I was responding and acting on instinct, setting my emotions aside and helping a person who needed my help. I look back and feel pleased that I made many good decisions that night, decisions I believe helped David survive. My son, though, seemed to take David's words more personally. As with most parents, children know little about their parent's work. Joshua never said anything to me about David's comments, but I think something within Joshua changed. If nothing else, it planted a seed that grew, as Joshua is now also an EMT.

I know it has been a very rough road for David and I am very happy to know that he is doing so well.

My closing comments for David are that I wish the best for him. He has been to hell and back and he has seemed to triumph over every obstacle thrown at him and he has thrived.

To this day, though, when I think back to that night, I still get very emotional.

CHAPTER 28:
Joseph D. Norcott, Sr.

My wife, daughter, and I had moved to Texas only two days before David's accident. The evening of September 3, 1998, David told us he had to run out for on an errand. Later, we heard a large number of sirens, but had no idea what had happened or that it was anything concerning David. We were curious, but nothing more.

About an hour later, an ambulance showed up at our door and a member of the crew handed us David's credentials. He told us that David had been in a terrible accident and that he was at Parkland Hospital in Dallas.

He told us that David's car and a van, going the opposite direction, had both drifted into the median and crashed head on. The impact was so intense that the engine of David's car was in his lap.

He told us that David had died about three times that night before being air lifted to Parkland.

I also learned that the van that hit David was driven by a woman and her adult daughter and that it was littered with empty beer cans. Unlike my son, the only injury mentioned about the two of them was one broken leg.

By the time we arrived at Parkland and I fully learned of David's condition and the circumstances surrounding the accident, I could feel my body temperature skyrocketing and my mind going to a very dark place. It was made even worse when I learned from his girlfriend that the argument was over a cat. When I learned this, I turned to stone and was very quiet.

My son is hovering between life and death because of a cat; my mind simply could not grasp this. Initially, they would not let me near David and I was in the waiting area feeling like a caged, wild animal. These horrible things had happened to my son and there I stood, helpless. It wasn't until late in the night that I was finally able to pull myself together and begin thinking more rationally.

I spent the night in the hospital while my wife and daughter returned home. The next day they both returned and my daughter stayed with David while my wife and I went down to the cafeteria to get something to eat.

When we returned to my daughter, she was visibly shaken. She told us that the doctors were trying to find my wife and me to discuss something important. Unable to do so, they told my daughter that she would have to sign the paperwork authorizing them to remove David's leg. It was terrible that she was put in that position, but the leg had to be removed and we all knew that from what we had been told.

The road ahead was difficult for both David and me. We both had to live with grief and regrets. I did my best to help David, and it was difficult for me to move back to the northeast, leaving him behind.

There were many difficult conversations between us as David struggled with drug and alcohol abuse. I did my best as his father to counsel him, but things between us were often tense.

We finally decided that we both just wanted to live in peace, we wanted the conflict between us to end. From that point on, we have had a good relationship and I care deeply about my son and his future.

I know he has become a part of several groups and become friends with many people who have helped him along this journey, and I am very grateful for them.

CHAPTER 29:

Joey Goss

It was April 20, 2010, a typical weekday morning. At the time, I lived about 30 minutes from my office and would take my son to school before heading to work. This particular morning, after dropping my son off at his school, I pulled into a nearby station to fill my truck with gas.

I inserted my credit card into the slot on the pump and it replied with "Please use another card." I knew the card to be good, so I went inside to the counter to get this resolved. As I waited in line, I could not help but notice, sitting there on the floor, this pitiful man with no legs. He had a blanket wrapped around him and was hunched and hunkered down, staring at his cell phone, with a numb look on his face.

I could not help but wonder why he was there and what had happened to him. But I needed gas and I needed to get to my office, so I let the thought drop out of my head.

I got to the counter, explained my credit card issue with the clerk and she told me to go out and try again. I did so, but my card was still rejected.

I returned to the clerk's counter, reviewed my issue with her and said, "Here's my card, I just want to fill up the gas tank in my truck." She said, "How much do you want to charge on your card?" I told her,

"I don't know, I just wanted to fill my truck!" She informed me she needed an actual amount to punch into her register screen.

I stood there frustrated, but my eyes could not help returning to the sad sight sitting there on the floor.

She finally told me to return to the pump and get my gas. I went out and was able to dispense my fuel. Once finished, I had to go back in the store to sign the receipt. On the way to the truck, I was given a message, "Go back, say hello to the man on the floor, and see how you can help him."

Not wishing to argue with The Lord, I stopped, pulled out my business card and wrote my private cell phone number on the back.

I walked in, went behind the counter and said to David, "Man, is there anything I can do to help you?"

David sadly replied, "No, the short bus is coming soon to get me."

It dawned on me that this man had no personal self-worth at all. He was probably at the end of his rope. Regardless, he took my card and I told him to call me if he thought I could help.

I fully expected to hear from him sometime during the day. Instead, I heard nothing.

Several months passed and I had all but forgotten about him, when in early September I got that fateful call from David. He was speaking so softly that I could just barely hear him. He said something like, "I'm calling you and I don't know why, but it is about over for me."

I could barely hear him but I realized he was trying to tell me that he was either about to die or was about to kill himself. I paused, let it all sink in, and replied, "Man, if you want me to help you, you are going to have to speak up because I can barely hear you."

He sounded so pitiful that I continued, "Listen, if you are going to kill yourself, tell me now. I'm happy to come over and work with you to find an answer to your situation. But I don't want to come over for nothing. If you want my help, just wait a few minutes. I'll come over to your place and we'll see if we can come up with something."

When I arrived at his apartment, David was sitting in his wheelchair, without his legs, looking at the door. I walked in to his small place and sat down to talk with him for a while.

It is not out of character for me to help someone, but my immediate thought was to find out if David was on the verge of suicide. If so, I would call a professional. If not, I could determine if I could help him. It is interesting how God teaches and grows both parties in these types of relationships. Once I realized David had resources, I began to think more about how I could help him regain his self-confidence.

I asked him what was going on and he rambled on for a while, a bit of a pity party, telling me all that had happened to him. I finally cut him off and said, "So, what can I do for you?"

He began by telling me that he had two storage lockers and a garage full of stuff. He explained that if the items could be moved, he could park his car in the garage and stop paying for the two lockers as well as his carport.

I assured him I could take care of it.

I realized that the reason this stuff was so important to him was because in his mind, he felt he really didn't have anything. He must have felt that his only worth in this world was those few items in those boxes. I discovered that those boxes would occupy no more than four or five square feet of floor space, yet, at this point in his life, this was everything to him.

I came back about a week later with a couple of people to help. We cleaned out the two lockers along with his garage. Over the next two to three years, I moved these same boxes from one location to the next with them finally ending up in the barn on my ranch property.

One day, years later, I finally asked David if there was anything in those boxes that he really wanted or needed. As David's confidence grew, his need for these possessions waned. He looked at me, smiled, and said, "No, not really. You can get rid of it all."

At this point in our relationship, I really had no idea where all of this ultimately would lead us both. I just knew he needed help, that he needed an injection of self-esteem. I did feel that he was probably not sustainable, that at any moment he could fall back to his prior life.

When I look back on it, there was something that I didn't even notice at the time. God was telling me that I needed to both help and teach David. I needed to help him put one foot in front of the other and move forward.

I was taken aback when David initially asked me for a job. I wasn't sure what I could do with him, but decided to see what I could make happen in my office. I talked to Kathy, my assistant, and we came up with a few tasks we thought David might be able to handle. It took time though, time for all of us to learn exactly where David was, where he needed to go, and then, how to help him get there.

The first step was purely physical. David wanted to come to work in his wheelchair. I told him he needed to start wearing his prosthetic legs again, that he needed to walk upright like a man. His response did not really surprise me; at first, he retreated to the safety of victimhood by saying, "They no longer fit and they hurt when I put them on."

It was not the easiest beginning having David in our office. There was an adjustment period for everyone. David was getting used to walking on his legs around an office. To ensure that he would get up and walk using his legs, I told my assistant to daily task him with retrieving items from one end of the office and bringing them to the other. He would literally bounce off the walls as he walked. One day, he took such a bad tumble that he knocked a hole in the plasterboard of the drywall with his head. Someone in the office came running to get me, telling me what had just happened. I looked at her and said, "Did he get up? Is he walking again? Then don't worry about it."

A small issue, unique to having David in the office, was that his metal legs would gouge into the toilet seats. Within a few weeks, the seats would be so rough and splintered that no one else would want to use them. So, I was constantly having the toilet seats replaced.

David was learning to be in an office and working a job again. All of us had to work with David to re-teach him to think in a linear, organized fashion. Things were difficult at first, but as David's confidence grew, so did his abilities and we would then increase his responsibilities.

Each time his world grew a little, he also expanded his safety zone; he would merely redraw the line of that zone. It was expanding, but the lines were always there. I knew he would reach a point where I could no longer challenge him. I knew, like a mother bird, I would need to push him out of the nest and force him to fly on his own. But that was a day I really did not want to arrive; yet, I also knew that the day was rapidly approaching. The last thing I wanted for David was to see him back behind that gas station counter, hunkered down over his phone, waiting for the short bus.

I finally put him on the front desk to greet and welcome clients and vendors. He was so friendly that everyone loved to stop and visit with him, but it reached the point that it could cause congestion in the lobby. But everyone seemed to love David, so I just relaxed.

As the various markets changed, so did the demand for housing. I was having to shrink my business and was making plans to move away for a couple of years, for various reasons. I knew I had to let David go, but I needed a plan for that as well.

David was getting very involved and enthusiastic about exercise, his various accomplishments at the YMCA, and he was also volunteering there. He mentioned to me that he was working on his certificate to be a training coach. I encouraged him to think more seriously about this and talk to the manager of the facility.

David asked me if I could be a sponsor at the "Y." In an attempt to approach this from every angle possible, I thought this might be a way to leverage a gift to the YMCA and, in return, the "Y" could give David more responsibility. I was hoping that there might be something we all could see as David's next step in life. David brought the YMCA's fundraiser to my office to provide the information. We both agreed that David was unique and a benefit to the YMCA. I'm not sure if the donation actually helped, but David ultimately began working at the YMCA.

The day I had to separate David from the company absolutely broke my heart. "I'm sorry David but I have run out of a spot here for you." I was upset and I know that he was upset as well. But I also knew that I was doing the right thing and that it was the best thing for David. I worried that a change this dramatic might cause him to fall back into the destructive behavior of his past so I kept in regular contact with him, encouraging him and assuring him that I would help him, no matter what.

It is how David has changed my life that amazes me most. I look at the world, and especially people, differently. My relationship with David has taught me compassion for others that I previously did not have. God has certainly "softened" my approach with those who are having difficulties in their lives.

I saw myself as a successful, complete man. I thought I had the world by the tail. I now realize that God did not set up my meeting with David to merely help David grow, it was also to help me grow.

God is good.

CHAPTER 30:

Kathy Johnston

I was Joey Goss' administrative assistant when he first encountered David at the gas station that fateful morning in April 2010. Joey came into the office and told me about this legless man to whom he had offered his help.

As good and helpful a man as Joey is, I think it took even him aback when David asked for a job. I remember Joey coming to me and saying, "Well, I'm going to hire this guy and I need you to help him get going." I replied, "We don't really have any positions open, what do you want him to do?" Joey said, "You just take him and have him help you."

"Joey, can you give me any guidance here? What do you want done?"

Joey replied, "Just have him help you get anything done that needs to be done. Give it to him and let him do it."

The first day David came into the office, he was so timid and reserved and he was so nervous about being there. I really wasn't sure how this would all work out, but I decided I would just trust Joey's judgement.

I looked around my office and gave David a few small tasks organizing paperwork.

Early on, I noticed David's special talent in speaking to people on the phone. When a vacancy opened up at the front desk of the office, I put him in that position. I told him, "David, you are the first person people will encounter when contacting Cheldan Homes, either by walking in the front door or by calling. Their impression of this company starts with you. When you start the conversation, I want you to smile, because they will be able to hear that in your voice. I want you to not only help the caller, I want you to make the caller feel good."

That is exactly what David did and he was excellent.

I can still hear him answering the phone, "GOOD MORNING! Thank you for calling Cheldan Homes. This is David Norcott. How can I assist you today?"

Joey was adamant that no calls dropped into a voicemail system and David ensured that never happened.

David has this beautiful charm and upbeat quality about him. He had a sincere willingness to help those who called and he did his very best to get each call to the right person. He took a lot of personal ownership and pride in handling those calls.

Many people commented to me that he had a beautiful voice and that he was so charming and helpful.

Early on, I could tell that at times, Joey was frustrated with David and his progress. But I think that once Joey realized that David was not "milking the situation" and that he was giving it his best, Joey let David take the time needed. I do not think Joey ever regretted hiring and helping David. It was a joy and inspiration to all of us to see how fast and how far he progressed.

For a while he also helped me organizing files. He would go to great depths to ensure that every required item was in each construction file. There was a check list of about 35 items that each file needed to contain. If something was missing, David would take the initiative to call the various contractors to obtain the paperwork necessary to complete the file.

One thing that especially impressed me about David is that he would write down absolutely everything I instructed him to do. He seemed to want to always keep my instructions handy for reference so that he did not make any mistakes.

David just did excellent work. I cannot say enough good things about him and his determination.

When David first started at Cheldan, he was using his prosthetic legs with the assistance of two canes. Early on I started encouraging him to try walking with only one cane. Eventually, it was something he accepted as a challenge from me, I think.

He was hesitant, at first, but he finally gave up one cane. I believe it was around the time he started participating in the various 5K and 10K races that he gave up the second cane.

Once he got rid of both canes, he was bound and determined not to use them again.

Our office was trying to get everyone together for a 5K run in Fort Worth. All of us encouraged David to participate. About this same time, my husband, Jim, was diagnosed with multiple myeloma, a blood cancer. I told Jim about the run and he said, "Tell David that if he'll do the race, I'll do it too!"

I delivered the message to David and I think that it was part of the reason David decided to participate.

Walking that race with David and watching the joy in him as he crossed the finish line will always be with me. He was so elated and proud of his accomplishment. He did not just sit back and bask in the glow, he pushed forward. After that first race, there was no stopping him. It seemed that there was nothing he could not do as he pursued race after race.

It was also very apparent the role that God played in David's life and, I think, in the lives of all who came in contact with David. This was especially obvious from God bringing Joey and David together as well as Joey extending his hand to David to help him. But it was David who took it as far as he did, and I do believe that this was a bit of a surprise to Joey.

It was such a blessing to all of us in the office to see the man that David has become.

David has a very Can-Do attitude. He sees the obstacles and challenges in life and he accepts them and moves forward anyway. He was, and is, an inspiration to me and to those in the office.

On a more personal level, David and I frequently had lunch together. As my husband Jim struggled to fight his cancer, David would always ask about him and provide comfort to me, "I will continue to pray for you and your family." It was the support I needed. David was such a blessing to me as I could comfortably express my grief to David about Jim's illness and how it was affecting me.

Confiding in people always includes risk. But I felt that there was nothing I couldn't tell David, nothing he couldn't understand and keep private. I felt safe with him and I think he felt the same way about me. About this time, he would tell me about his personal struggle with his two children, his wanting to form a relationship with them.

I kept telling him, "You just have to keep trying, keep reaching out to them without an agenda. It will all happen in God's time."

I appreciate David's exuberance for life and I often wonder how I can manifest those same emotions and attitudes in my own life.

One weekend, I decided to see what daily life must be like for David, trying to understand his life. So, I spent a part of my weekend at home doing normal tasks while on my knees. I now better understand the challenges he faces when merely brushing his teeth or washing his hands. Another thing I tried was vacuuming the rug. I didn't last long, but I became even more impressed with David's grit, determination, and positive attitude.

He told me once about how creative he had to be when a light bulb in his apartment needed to be changed. A simple task to me required considerable innovation by David.

I think what impresses me most is that David never used his physical limitations as an excuse and he NEVER played the victim card. No matter the task, he found a way to accomplish it and made it happen.

One last thing: he a very sweet, thoughtful man. I too thank God for bringing David into my life.

CHAPTER 31:
Andrew & Glenda Bashor

"If you were standing in a swimming pool and the person next to you was drowning, wouldn't you reach over and help him?"
- Andrew Bashor

We were David's next-door neighbors in the apartment complex. This was where David moved after his marriage to Lecia ended. While getting to know him, it seemed as if everything in his life had gone wrong. He recently separated from his wife, he was losing his house, he had car problems, and, of course, his physical limitations. It seemed that he just needed a little assistance. At first, I simply helped him retrieve items from his house before it was foreclosed upon.

We wanted David to thrive, to be independent. We knew he was suffering and we couldn't just stand by, watch, and do nothing.

As he continued spiraling downward, we did our best to provide him with love and support. At times that would be helping him with issues in his apartment, issues with the management of the apartment complex, problems with his car, and at other times, taking him to AA meetings.

After David bottomed out and decided to throw away the drugs and alcohol, he locked himself in his apartment to detoxify. He was very much like a drowning man. We simply did what needed to be done. We merely did our best to grab him and help pull him up.

We prayed regularly for David, and slowly, very slowly, God brought about the change for which we prayed.

We included David in our holiday and family celebrations, making sure he was not alone. As a friend, you never know where these types of kindnesses will lead or how they might help.

He was a good guy, a good friend. We had the movie *Avatar*, about a paraplegic man, and David must have come over 4 times to watch it with us. I'm sure it planted some seeds in his consciousness.

After joining a Christian organization that responds to disasters and helps those in need, we moved to Tennessee in early 2011.

In the spring of 2012, David contacted us saying he would be driving to Maryland to his son's high school graduation. He asked if he could spend the night at our house. Of course, we were thrilled that he was taking on this solo trip and more than happy to host him.

When we left Texas, David was still using his wheelchair 100% of the time and he was still addicted to drugs and alcohol. When he arrived at our home, he was walking on his prosthetic legs and was clean and sober. It was a spectacular event for all of us.

We walked out to greet him as he pulled into our driveway. He simply got out of his car and walked toward us like any other friend of ours. It nearly brought me to tears as I watched him. His balance on his legs was amazing. He had developed extraordinary core strength and was even able to walk without using his canes.

It was fully seeing all that God had done in David's life that filled our hearts that day. It was seeing how much he had progressed that was so wonderful. We knew there were numerous people who helped David succeed in his journey and we were grateful for those people as well.

Back in Texas there were numerous times where the chair created problems for him, either by losing a wheel or by simply not functioning, and there David would be, stranded. At times, he would not be able to even get back into the chair. This then forced him to spend more time using his prosthetic legs. Through this, he developed more core strength and became more independent

Looking back, I don't think he fully realized what a detriment to his progress his wheelchair had actually been. Now, here at our home in Tennessee, he was walking and thriving. I know that he had brought his chair with him in the car, but I don't recall him using it while at our house.

Glenda: "It was mostly Andrew who cared for and helped David. The times I would go to his apartment, it was sad to see all that was happening, but I worked to focus on the progress David was making in his life. He slowly found solutions to issues in his apartment that prevented him from living his life. I focused on those accomplishments rather than on the sadness of the situation."

We also have such great respect for David's ability to talk to people and to win them over, affecting changes in their lives as well.

Andrew: "I was raised to help others. After a storm, my father would take me out to drive around our town, looking for those who might need help, such as someone stuck in a ditch or whose car might be overwhelmed by snow, and help them. This is just who Glenda and I are. We see a need and we help as we can. It isn't about being a hero, it isn't really about doing anything special; it is simply a friend helping a friend."

After helping David out of the water and then his realizing that he could breathe on his own, everything seemed to come together for him. He discovered what he could do and how he could make it all happen. It has all been absolutely amazing. It is a testament to how much God loves each of us.

CHAPTER 32:

Mark Ashford

I first met David about eighteen years ago, while working for Hanger Clinic, where I am a prosthetist. At that time, David had already been fitted for prosthetics by another company, yet it seemed to me, at that time, that David did not yet have the commitment necessary to live a productive life wearing them.

Let me be clear: Adapting to life as an above-the-knee (bi-lateral or both legs) amputee is a tough road, one requiring a lot of persistence and tenacity. At our initial meeting, I did not think that David was quite yet at that point, but this is common for many amputees as it takes time to fully realize the level of effort required to thrive with prosthetics.

The previous company started him with full-length legs and, not surprisingly to me, he was failing at it. My recommendation to him was to take a giant "step" backward so that he could begin building strength and balance. To do this, though, would require switching back to what are called "stubbies" which are a very short prosthesis. I knew this step was necessary for David to succeed with the longer legs, but I also suspected he would be very resistant to this change. I also knew he would eventually need to move into C-legs (computer assisted legs). His first legs merely had hydraulic knees, this is comparable to walking on stilts, whereas C-legs have knees that can be calibrated to the patient's gait and can compensate for a variety of surfaces.

As David continued to gain strength from walking using the stubbies, we began setting targets for him to advance to longer and longer legs.

Yes, David could be very hard-headed at times, but like most people, David wanted to be the same height he was before the accident, so I understood why he would get frustrated. My goal, like his, was for him to get there; we just had very different schedules. If he was going to succeed with the C-legs, he was going to have to be physically ready for them as well.

As much as I wanted David to succeed, it is much like working with an alcoholic. Things only change when the client is ready for them to change. I could only sit back and wait for him to realize this as well.

I think David had become overly dependent upon others to help him, and living his life in a wheelchair fed into that.

"Playing the victim is an easy way out of many problems in life."

Wearing prosthetic legs, especially for an above-the-knee amputee, is one of the most difficult things a person can experience. I understand why people give up. It takes a special person with determination to make it work. As I would learn over time, David was one of those special people.

When David first started working with the parallel bars, he would make one pass on the bars and end up soaked in sweat. It takes about 600% more effort for a bilateral amputee to walk than a non-amputee.

The more he walked, the easier it became for him. I was encouraged with his progress but not really cognizant, at that time, of just how bad things were in his private life.

I really was not as aware of his drug and alcohol issues as I probably should have been. I never seemed to smell any booze on him nor notice any specific impairment in his behavior.

During the time David was "bottoming out," he rarely came to the clinic as he almost never wore his legs. For me it was a case of "out of sight, out of mind." Also, some amputees simply do not often use their legs and therefore, need very little follow up. I assumed the same to be true of David, so I had no real idea of just how badly his life was going.

Clearly, Joey Goss entering his life made a huge impact. Even though I told David many of the same things Joey said to him, he seemed to actually hear it when Joey said it. First of all, you must regularly wear the legs, even if it is only to put them on and stand up for a short while, but you must do this every day. This allows the tissue to become pressure tolerant.

When Joey told David that he needed to leave his wheelchair at home and wear his legs into work, David took this to heart and did as he was told. This, in turn, led him to return to Hanger Clinic for further fine tuning of his legs.

Just as with wearing the legs, I would often challenge and encourage David to do more, to break out of his usual boundaries, but, probably because of our long history, I was often not the best person to challenge him.

This probably became the most obvious when David's co-worker asked him to participate in the Fort Worth Turkey Trot. I would never have suggested that to David at that time. Not because I did not think he could do it, but because I thought, based on past experience, David would just smile and dismiss the idea.

I knew this race would be a huge challenge for David, both physically and mentally. At that time, he was still walking with his canes. After telling me his intent to walk in the race, he asked if I could help him prepare.

I suggested David come to my office every Monday afternoon around 4pm. From there, we would just begin by walking around the neighborhood. It was quite warm outside, so I would grab two bottles of water and off we would go.

The challenges come from the variety of surfaces David would have to navigate on this 5K walk. Each surface requires slightly different techniques and David wanted to master those long before actually arriving on the course.

It was tiring work for David as he prepared. Sometimes we would just stop and lean against a tree and other times we would find a bench or stoop on which to sit.

It was taxing for both of us, but David seemed to be committed to reaching this goal, proving to both of us that he could actually make this happen. I wanted to do everything possible to help him.

It was wonderful to see him rise to the challenge of this race. I felt that even if he did not finish it, he would still have made an amazing accomplishment. By simply making the effort, he would shatter the boundaries and limits he had placed upon himself. The best part was that he had fun with it.

From this experience, I realized that I needed to spend more time challenging and encouraging all of my patients.

Amputees face daily challenges that are often difficult for able-bodied people to comprehend. As an example, David once told me that he was afraid to cook, he was afraid of the fire and heat and the possibility that he might spill hot food on himself. Spilling food onto the floor is also a fear because of the difficulties for an amputee to clean it up.

I tasked him to start "cooking" without actually cooking. I told him to go through all of the motions of cooking without using any heat. I told him to use plastic dishes and imaginary foods and simply go through the motions of cooking until he became comfortable and confident in the process. He would cook with neither fire nor food.

Every year Hanger Clinic hosts a bi-lateral Boot Camp. At this camp, we challenge our patients to get out of the wheelchair, get off their pain medications, and move forward in life.

I invited David to attend several times over the years, but he always seemed to have one excuse or another. Finally, about two years ago, he did attend. I think he got a lot out of the experience, made many good friends and helped others struggling with their own life challenges.

Over the years, David and I have developed a good relationship. Ultimately, if you do not reach a point where you can laugh about your disability, you will just cry all the time. Initially, David somberly addressed his challenges. Now he is able to laugh and joke about it. With that new attitude comes the ability to make greater strides and progress and watch your internal barriers and limitation diminish.

I'm sure he still has those days when he is frustrated and discouraged, but, guess what? We all have those days.

I want David to be as strong and active as possible, because all of us, regardless of our limitations, will age and will lose the ability to enjoy life in the same way as now.

I've watched David go from merely "existing" in his life to thriving, living life to its fullest.

CHAPTER 33:
David On David

"Nine years ago, at the beginning of my becoming awake, conscious, and sober, I just wanted to see the light at the top of the hole I was in. I also wanted to see from whence the light was coming. Now, I am flying next to it. I actually got more than I initially asked. I know now that this is how God provides for us. To fully experience God, you must also fully trust Him.

The David before the accident was broken from childhood. I obsessed about the pain in my life and lived in my various "escapisms." I never confronted and dealt with any of my emotional issues. I eschewed obstacles in life and hid within my emotions and on various drugs. Once becoming sober, unable to hide within a bottle, I finally started facing these challenges.

Upon leaving the rehab hospital, the staff told me, "Your emotions will now feel like a bad sunburn, raw, painful, and un-medicated, *but* they will heal." I did not realize until then that I did not have to give my pain authority over me, any longer.

Before all of these events, I was living *my* story. Now, I am living *God's* plan for me. It is surrendering to God and His Path for my life. I do not always do the right thing, but I keep re-evaluating, and returning to my path.

It is nothing I ever thought it was going to be, and now that I feel that I am on the other side, it is more than I could have ever imagined.

Right now, my highest aspirations are merely the starting point of what God will fully reveal for me. I have done more for myself and for others in the last nine years than I did in the prior 42 years of my life. I am trying to help others and add value to my community. My sobriety has been very successful because I focus on the light.

I have more than I could ever wish for.

The David before was self-seeking, self-serving, and self-promoting. If there was nothing in it for me, I would not participate. Now I try to think more of others than of myself. Now I do things without anyone even knowing and I receive even more blessings from God.

A few years ago, I was blessed to hear and meet Nick Vujicic. For those who have never had the honor of meeting him or hearing his message, Nick was born without arms and legs. A native of Australia, he now travels the world delivering his special message of love, hope and determination. A friend of mine told me that Nick was speaking at her church here in the Dallas area and she invited me to attend. After Nick's presentation, as I was leaving the auditorium, a security guard touched my shoulder and asked, "Would you like to meet Nick?" I didn't have to think very long to answer, "Of course. I would love to meet him."

I was taken to an area behind the stage and introduced to Nick. After a warm welcome, Nick said the most extraordinary thing to me. He said, "It must have been very difficult for you. You once had legs and now you don't. You had to grieve their loss and refocus your life. On the other hand, I have never had either arms or legs and therefore have never known anything different."

Wow, what a statement. I don't think many people can look at Nick and expect him to feel sorry for them. But I have found this same attitude in many people who daily face health challenges. They tend to find the good in their lives and dwell upon that, they focus on what they can do rather than what they cannot. They are among the happiest of those in our society, when society would assume they would be the least happy.

At the beginning of this book, I wrote down a quote by Sgt. Johnny Jones, a veteran who lost both of his legs in combat, "People ask how I can stay so positive after losing my legs. I simply ask how they stay so negative with theirs."

When I stopped focusing my life on just me, when I stopped trying to manipulate others for my own destructive ends, the world suddenly became a brighter, friendlier place. Of course, the world did not change, I did.

I pray that everyone finds their place in this world. I pray they seek joy instead of misery.

And always, always remember these two things: "It is never too late to change your life, to do right, or to make a change or a choice," and "The answer to every unasked question is 'No'."

PART VI:

Ascension

"Behold! I tell you a mystery. We shall not all sleep,
but we shall all be changed"
1 Corinthians 15:51

CHAPTER 34:
A Grievous End

Saturday, July 31, 2021

This is like any other Saturday with Kinsey at my side while at my job at the Benbrook YMCA. I feel great and have a good time welcoming and chatting with the members as they come in for their morning workouts.

Toward the end of the day, I seem a little more tired than usual, but I brush it off and go home. "A good night's sleep is all I need."

Sunday, August 1, 2021

Still feeling a l little odd, I start my day and run a few errands. While out, I run into a YMCA friend, Renee. We chat for a while and I begin realizing just how fatigued I really am. Maybe an afternoon nap is in my future, something I rarely do.

Monday, August 2, 2021

Could I have The Covid? Nah, impossible, I was one of the first people to receive the vaccine in Texas. I'm safe. As the day progresses, I realize I am developing more and more of the most common symptoms of covid, including congestion in my chest. I drive to a local pharmacy and get the covid test. Surprisingly, it comes back positive.

Although the staff recommends I go to a hospital, I know the data states that the vaccine minimizes the symptoms of covid, so I decide instead to just go home and rest.

Once home, I call several friends and arrange for them to bring me food and take Kinsey for her walks for the next several days. I'm certain I will recover quickly.

I also call Renee, who I ran into both on Saturday and on Sunday, and let her know my situation, in case she also feels the need to get tested for covid.

Wednesday, August 4, 2021

I'm actually feeling quite well. It appears I am overcoming this virus as easily as the reports have stated. Hopefully, I'll be back to work on Saturday.

Thursday, August 5, 2021

Damn! *I CAN'T BREATHE!* Each breath is a struggle. Poor Kinsey knows something is wrong as she hovers near me. I finally reach for my phone and dial 911, asking for an ambulance.

One arrives shortly and the paramedics load me and Kinsey into the back of the van. The paramedics quickly get to work giving me oxygen, starting an IV, and communicating my situation to the local hospital.

From my own time as a paramedic, I know by the behavior of the men that my situation is dire. I can't help but reflect on the irony of being a paramedic and that I now feel as if I may die in the back of a bus upon which I once may have worked myself.

Before we even arrive at the hospital, God reaches down and takes me into His arms.

EPILOGUE

"Let us be silent that we may hear the whisper of God"
– Ralph Waldo Emerson

I hope the reader has found David's journey as amazing and inspiring as it was for me to write. Just when you think everything bad has happened, something new hit him. Having also dealt with serious health issues and having spent months in various hospitals, I can relate to David's anguish and desire to be free and independent from care. I can also relate to his being tethered to equipment to function in daily life. My issues are small compared to what David endured, but my admiration and ability to relate to his struggles made this book a very special project to me.

As I have read, re-read, and edited this book, I realized the number of times David mentioned that he had not fully dealt with his emotional problems. In retrospect, it almost seems to be a cry for help. Even if I had picked up on it at the time of the interviews, there was really nothing I could do other than to suggest a therapist. I do wish I noticed these comments at that time, though. There were many stumbling blocks in getting this book written and published. I can only speculate that these unresolved emotional issues may have contributed to those impediments.

In spite of my doubts about some parts of the story, I cannot help but commend David on accepting the hand he had been dealt, rising up from the ashes of his life and attacking it with full force.

Only briefly did he roll over and play the victim. Quickly, he took control of the situation and rose above it. In all the time I knew him, he might talk about some of the challenges he faced, but he never whined or complained. As he commented in one of the interviews about his father, "My father did everything he had to do to make me do everything I had to do by never letting me play the victim card."

I remember once being in a restaurant with David when he excused himself to go to the restroom. I watched him on his prosthetic legs awkwardly navigating the room. As my eyes shifted back, I noticed a girl at the next table taking her seat. Across her sweatshirt it read, "The Struggle is Real." I almost laughed and thought about asking her to join us so that she could tell David about her "real struggle."

I often think of a quote from Gen. Chuck Yeager when I think of David:

"You do what you can for as long as you can, and when you finally can't, you do the next best thing. You back up but you don't give up." – *Gen. Chuck Yeager*

We have all dealt with challenges in our lives. We have or will all encounter those defining moments when our life's expectations and plans are challenged by God's own plans for us. We can give up and give into the "struggle" or we can move forward. Spiritual growth only comes through pain and suffering. It is vital that we all move on to the "next best thing."

David's story also highlights the magnitude of power our own attitudes have in our lives. When David's attitude changed, the entire world seemed to change. This is true for all of us.

When David received his Canine Companions service dog "Kinsey," I was invited to a breakfast for the graduates. At that time, the Honorable Judge Edward Kinkaede spoke about those in the graduating class. He mentioned that he had spoken to David about his accident and how David now viewed it. David replied, "It was a blessing." Judge Kinkaede commented that he was not sure that he could be so magnanimous if he was faced with such a challenge.

The reality is that none of us know how we will respond to challenges in life until those challenges manifest themselves. You can choose to merely *exist* in life or you can choose to *thrive*, regardless or your personal circumstances.

Speaking from my own experience as a heart failure patient, I am far more aware of others with life-limiting health issues or parents who must face those issues at the side of their children. I may be frustrated, at times, with my situation and my limitations, but I can quickly find others around me also coping with challenges. David was one of those people in my life. No, I would never think of wearing a shirt stating "The Struggle is Real" even though I do face challenges daily. I know that there are too many around me who face far greater challenges than I will ever have to face and they walk proud, erect, and positive in the face of those obstacles. It is my decision and my choice how I deal with my limitations, just as it was David's.

I recently heard a quote from a woman battling cancer. I think her words sum up the spirit I find in so many people facing overwhelming odds: "It is important that everyone knows I am so much more than just the bad things that have happened to me."

Amen

OTHER BOOKS BY THOMAS MARTIN

Available on Amazon and on TMartinBooks.com

God's Love: My Life as a Service Dog

One Percent: My Journey Overcoming Heart Disease

Just Do This One Thing: A Guide to Chronic Good Health

More Bang for Your Bucks:
An Insider's Guide to Basic Financial Decisions

Ten Steps to Reversing Autism:
A Natural, Organic, Dietary Approach

No More Heart Attacks:
A 10 Step Protocol to Reversing Heart Disease

So, Why Did You Become a Mason:
Travelers Taking Their First Steps Seeking Light